Building Beautiful Wooden Chests

Building Beautiful Wooden
CHESTS

GARTH GRAVES

POPULAR WOODWORKING BOOKS
CINCINNATI, OHIO
www.popularwoodworking.com

READ THIS IMPORTANT SAFETY NOTICE To prevent accidents, keep safety in mind while you work. Use the safety guards installed on power equipment; they are for your protection. When working on power equipment, keep fingers away from saw blades, wear safety goggles to prevent injuries from flying wood chips and sawdust, wear headphones to protect your hearing, and consider installing a dust vacuum to reduce the amount of airborne sawdust in your woodshop. Don't wear loose clothing, such as neckties or shirts with loose sleeves, or jewelry, such as rings, necklaces or bracelets, when working on power equipment, and tie back long hair to prevent it from getting caught in your equipment. The author and editors who compiled this book have tried to make the contents as accurate and correct as possible. Plans, illustrations, photographs and text have been carefully checked. All instructions, plans and projects should be carefully read, studied and understood before beginning construction. Due to the variability of local conditions, construction materials, skill levels, etc., neither the author nor Popular Woodworking Books assumes any responsibility for any accidents, injuries, damages or other losses incurred resulting from the material presented in this book.

METRIC CONVERSION CHART

TO CONVERT	TO	MULTIPLY BY
Inches	Centimeters	2.54
Centimeters	Inches	0.4

Building Beautiful Wooden Chests. Copyright © 1999 by Garth Graves. Manufactured in the United States of America. All rights reserved. No part of this book may be reproduced in any form or by any electronic or mechanical means including information storage and retrieval systems without permission in writing from the publisher, except by a reviewer, who may quote brief passages in a review. Published by Popular Woodworking Books, an imprint of F&W Publications, Inc., 1507 Dana Avenue, Cincinnati, Ohio 45207. (800) 289-0963. First edition.

Other fine Popular Woodworking Books are available from your local bookstore or direct from the publisher.

Visit our Web site at www.popularwoodworking.com for information on more resources for woodworkers.

03 02 01 00 99   5 4 3 2 1

Library of Congress Cataloging-in-Publication Data

Graves, Garth
    Building beautiful wooden chests / by Garth Graves.
        p.   cm.
    Includes index.
    ISSBN 1-55870-487-6 (alk. paper)
    1. Furniture making. 2. Chests. I. Title.
TT197.G685   1999
684.1'6—dc21   98-47133
                                                      CIP

Editor: Karen A. Spector
Production editor: Christine K. Doyle
Production coordinator: Erin Boggs
Designer: Angela Lennert Wilcox

DEDICATION

To my wife—my VP of detail.

ACKNOWLEDGMENTS

A special thanks to the craftspeople whose chest projects made this book possible. Each contributor was working on a deadline (for a client or for themselves), and yet they took the time to share their product, their approach and their specialty with those just entering the craft and with the rest of us who are still learning.

To those who helped in the search for chest builders, those who were invited to contribute but couldn't because the timing was wrong and to those who erroneously thought they had too little to share, I say in the words of Bob Stevenson, or project twelve fame (not Robert Lewis, although he could have said it): "Sharing is what it's all about."

TABLE OF CONTENTS

Introduction
page 10

The Evolution and
History of the Chest
page 11

Gallery of Beautiful
Wooden Chests
page 65

PROJECT ONE

Deacon's Bench

CAROL REED

page 25

Three Views
page 26

Design Detail
page 27

Work in Progress
page 28

Variation
page 31

The Builder's Thoughts
page 32

Questions and Answers
page 33

PROJECT TWO

Rustic Blanket Chest

MARTIN PREVOSTO

page 35

Three Views
page 36

Design Details
page 37

Work in Progress
page 38

Variations
page 40

The Builder's Thoughts
page 41

Questions and Answers
page 41

PROJECT THREE

Spanish Cedar Chest

GARTH GRAVES

page 43

Three Views
page 44

Design Details
page 45

Work in Progress
page 46

Variations
page 49

The Builder's Thoughts
page 50

Questions and Answers
page 50

PROJECT FOUR

Craftsman Chairside Chest

GARTH GRAVES

page 51

Three Views
page 52

Design Details
page 53

Work in Progress
page 54

Variations
page 56

The Builder's Thoughts
page 57

Questions and Answers
page 58

PROJECT FIVE

Japanese Tansu

JOHN GILLIS

page 59

Three Views
page 60

Design Details
page 61

Work in Progress
page 62

Variations
page 64

The Builder's Thoughts
page 73

Questions and Answers
page 74

PROJECT SIX

Shaker Chest of Drawers

MIKE TRAUPEL

page 75

Three Views
page 76

Design Details
page 77

Work in Progress
page 78

Variation
page 80

The Builder's Thoughts
page 81

Questions and Answers
page 82

TABLE OF CONTENTS continued

PROJECT SEVEN

Lingerie Chest

STAN PIECHOTA

page 83

Three Views

page 84

Design Details

page 85

Work in Progress

page 86

Variations

page 88

The Builder's Thoughts

page 89

Questions and Answers

page 89

PROJECT EIGHT

Coin Collector's Chest

GARY MCNEIL

page 91

Two Views

page 92

Design Details

page 93

Work in Progress

page 94

Variation

page 96

The Builder's Thoughts

page 97

Questions and Answers

page 98

PROJECT NINE

Cigar Humidor

RYAN COWELL

page 99

Three Views

page 100

Design Details

page 101

Work in Progress

page 102

Variations

page 104

The Builder's Thoughts

page 105

Questions and Answers

page 105

PROJECT TEN

Jewelry Chest

RYAN COWELL

page 107

Three Views

page 108

Design Details

page 109

Work in Progress

page 110

Variation

page 112

The Builder's Thoughts

page 113

Questions and Answers

page 114

PROJECT ELEVEN

Williamsburg Gentleman's Tool Chest

ANDREW MCPHERSON

page 115

Three Views

page 116

Design Details

page 117

Work in Progress

page 118

Variations

page 121

The Builder's Thoughts

page 122

Questions and Answers

page 123

PROJECT TWELVE

Eighteenth Century Federal Sideboard

ROBERT STEVENSON

page 124

Three Views

page 125

Design Details

page 126

Work in Progress

page 127

Variations

page 129

The Builder's Thoughts

page 130

Questions and Answers

page 131

INDEX

page 133

Introduction

This is an idea book bringing together collectively examples of what is being done individually. It is a look at the way craftspeople approach building beautiful wooden chests.

Those invited to build a chest for the book were selected for their craftsmanship, sense of design and use of materials. Each contributor possesses the ability to translate his or her skills and talents into beautiful chests.

Starting with a look at chests from their humble beginning and at some of the highlights along the road of development, the pages that follow will showcase present-day interpretations in design and style through twelve chest projects produced by ten woodworkers. Most followed the more classic structure of past successes, and a few offer a new twist on a very basic piece of furniture.

The Who

Artisans, craftsmen, woodworkers and furniture builders were invited to share their objectives, approaches and results. A Question and Answer section explores each particular person and his or her project.

The What

You will find in the pages that follow a collection that includes chests, chest-over-drawers, a chest/bench, chests of drawers, and chests for coins, cigars, jewelry, tools and dinnerware. In these projects you will find various methods, techniques and approaches by ten different builders from ten different perspectives.

The When

A look at early chests shows the evolution of this oldest furniture form, which began as a hollow log and developed over numerous eras. You will see some prime examples in today's museum pieces.

The Why

You will find a close-up look at the product, the approach and the builder from concept through design and construction. These ideas are for you to use in whatever you build. A variation of each project is also included to jump-start your thinking toward some future project.

You already know, or are becoming more proficient in, design, joinery and finishing. This idea book will hopefully foster or boost, instill or awaken a new approach. At least you should come away with new ideas to supplement your signature style and craftsmanship. Take a look at some of your fellow woodworkers building beautiful wooden chests.

Enjoy.

The Evolution and History of the Chest

The Evolution of the Chest

The new millennium approaches at breakneck speed, and with it will come almost unimaginable changes in everything we do. We are currently in the computer-driven Information Age. Back in the Industrial Age, innovation also had a profound impact on the way people lived. Even in periods when time moved more slowly, discovery and development still brought about major changes to life and living. The further back we look, the further these changes are removed from the modern technology which we take for granted.

Like the rich figuring of wood from a tree that struggled to survive, the craftsman's creativity and inventiveness were sharpened and honed during both good periods and bad. There were alternating times of oppression and free expression and some heavy-handed class distinction between the possessions of aristocrats and peasants, particularly furniture.

The furniture piece that's been around the longest, the chest, was naturally subjected to more pendulum swings than newer types of furniture, but it has survived and is the origin of all casework furniture. To design and make something both simple and beautiful shows a craftsman's mettle. The chest is inherently simple.

A brief evolution of the chest follows. This is just a sampling of past chests; it reveals in two pages an example of the variety of chests from plain to decorative.

Coffer Chests

A coffer chest is any shell for storage. It can be a dowry chest, a marriage chest, a blanket chest or a toy chest. When built to be transported, it can be a trunk or campaign chest or a captain's or sea chest.

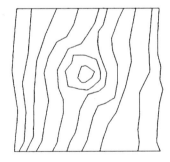

A hollow stump made a good early chest.

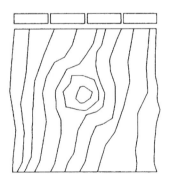

Adding a planked lid, the hollow tree section and crest made a good seat.

Six-plank chests were limited by plank widths. Edge-joined planks got bigger and heavier. A lid makes it a good bench.

Casework Chests

Chests evolved into casework chests when openings moved from a lift lid to the front. Examples of this include a small commode, a full chest of drawers, a chest-on-chest, a dresser, a bureau, a desk.

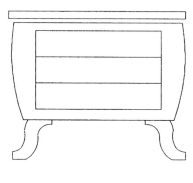

A low chest became a commode (1600) or small chest for the parlor. The water bowl was added later when the commode arrived on the bedroom scene. The bombe sides flourished on this small chest.

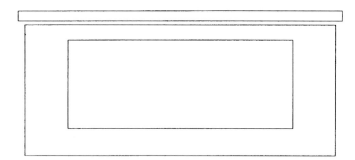

A fixed lid chest with front access marked the beginning of casework chests. The fixed top allowed for use as a table or a bed.

Larger casework chests evolved into the chest-of-drawers, providing more orderly storage of possessions.

As chests were getting larger and heavier, they were prone to splitting. The frame and panel design (1300) added some decoration while reducing weight and stress.

The chest-on-chest, or tallboy in England, became popular in America for 100 more years as the highboy.

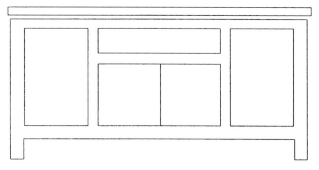

The drawer (1500) was just a chest inside a chest. This led to drawers, then to the dresser. The dresser was an early sideboard used for carving, dishing and serving food (i.e. "dressing" food).

History of the Chest

To protect their valuable possessions, our ancestors buried them underground, covered them with rocks or stashed them in a hollow tree along with the squirrel's winter nut supply. The tree concept took hold and evolved into hollowing a length of tree trunk and adding a planked lid to make the early coffer chest.

The coffer's lid became a sturdy seat. As possessions accumulated, a longer chest held more and became a bench, and larger chests served as tables and beds.

During this design evolution, access moved from a lift or hinged lid to a front panel or doors. In this way contents could be fetched without disturbing things stacked on top (much like a workbench). This front-access chest became the body for a fall-front desk, a drawer chest, then for raised, open shelves such as a cupboard or cabinet.

Throughout the ages, civilizations developed a variety of wooden chests in designs ranging from crude to highly ornamental. Some were adorned for pharaohs, emperors, popes and kings.

Like a skipping stone across a pond, the following time line touches only a few examples to illustrate the development of furniture design. The examples that follow come from classic chests displayed in today's museums.

2000 B.C.–A.D. 1200

Chests from Egypt, Mesopotamia, Assyria and the designs developed for Greek and Roman aristocracy were the forerunners of modern furniture. In medieval times, chests were far more functional than ornate. During the Middle Ages, few people had possessions to be harbored. Some people, however, tended to move around a lot and the chest was practical for storing and carrying their goods. Chests also provided a place to sit after arriving at the destination.

Furniture development didn't progress, but, in fact, almost had to begin again following the Middle Ages. More people in many different cultures were beginning to accumulate possessions. Those possessions needed to be stored and protected.

In the cathedrals of the Byzantine kingdoms, rulers pampered themselves with finely crafted chests. Most ordinary people were kept from receiving their full furniture entitlement until Henry VIII's division with Rome in the early 1500s. Then, gradually, availability of furniture began to extend to the masses. The Industrial Revolution ushered in an era of greater supply of furniture at lower cost.

Canopic chests were typically built with skids (sledge), and this example has a cambered lid flanked by rectangular ends. Canopic chests were buried in the tombs of the people of Ancient Egypt; the chests held canopic jars, in which were placed the mummified organs of the deceased.

Canopic Chest
CORBIS/Gianni Dagli Orti

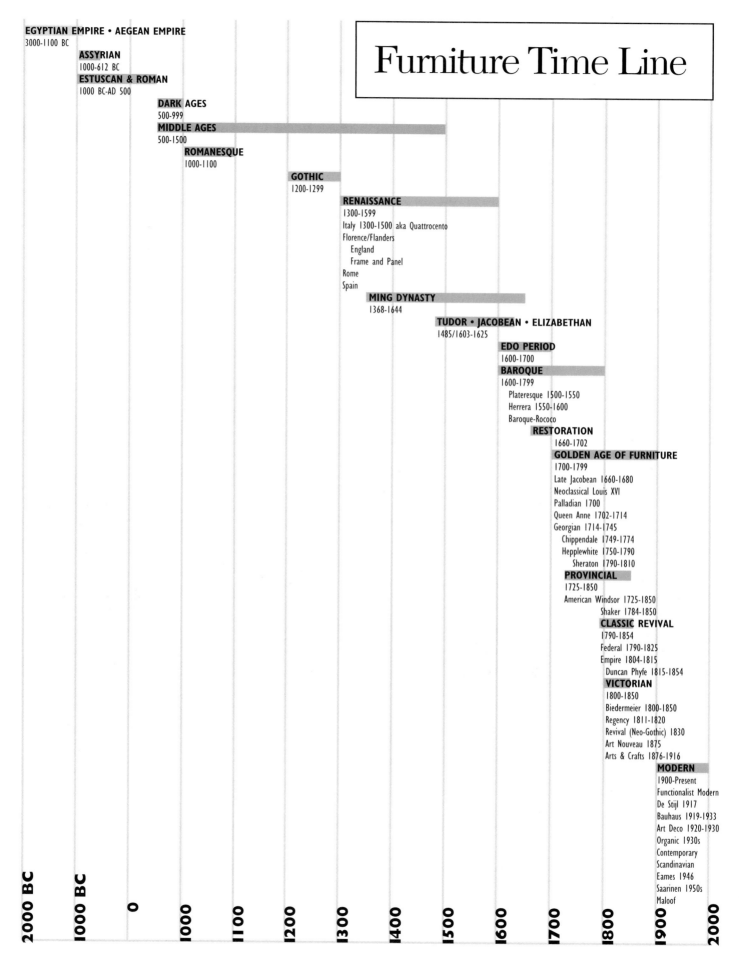

Furniture Time Line

EGYPTIAN EMPIRE • AEGEAN EMPIRE
3000-1100 BC

ASSYRIAN
1000-612 BC

ESTUSCAN & ROMAN
1000 BC-AD 500

DARK AGES
500-999

MIDDLE AGES
500-1500

ROMANESQUE
1000-1100

GOTHIC
1200-1299

RENAISSANCE
1300-1599
Italy 1300-1500 aka Quattrocento
Florence/Flanders
   England
   Frame and Panel
Rome
Spain

MING DYNASTY
1368-1644

TUDOR • JACOBEAN • ELIZABETHAN
1485/1603-1625

EDO PERIOD
1600-1700

BAROQUE
1600-1799
   Plateresque 1500-1550
   Herrera 1550-1600
   Baroque-Rococo

RESTORATION
1660-1702

GOLDEN AGE OF FURNITURE
1700-1799
Late Jacobean 1660-1680
Neoclassical Louis XVI
Palladian 1700
Queen Anne 1702-1714
Georgian 1714-1745
   Chippendale 1749-1774
   Hepplewhite 1750-1790
    Sheraton 1790-1810

PROVINCIAL
1725-1850
American Windsor 1725-1850
   Shaker 1784-1850

CLASSIC REVIVAL
1790-1854
Federal 1790-1825
Empire 1804-1815
   Duncan Phyfe 1815-1854

VICTORIAN
1800-1850
Biedermeier 1800-1850
Regency 1811-1820
Revival (Neo-Gothic) 1830
Art Nouveau 1875
Arts & Crafts 1876-1916

MODERN
1900-Present
Functionalist Modern
De Stijl 1917
Bauhaus 1919-1933
Art Deco 1920-1930
Organic 1930s
Contemporary
Scandinavian
Eames 1946
Saarinen 1950s
Maloof

2000 BC   **1000 BC**   **0**   **1000**   **1100**   **1200**   **1300**   **1400**   **1500**   **1600**   **1700**   **1800**   **1900**   **2000**

1300–1400s

While much of the Western world was still in the Middle Ages, Eastern cultures adorned palaces and temples with the finest of woodworking crafts. Renowned for glueless joinery, many eastern examples of altars and other furnishings are classic studies in joinery techniques and showpieces in the world's museums. This was especially true during the Ming Dynasty (1368–1644) which exhibited a renewed dedication to excellence in workmanship and materials.

Gothic tracery was carved into chests and other furniture. The Renaissance encompassed many European centers, providing a varied approach in chest decoration and construction.

This Gothic tracery style from France indicates an early effort, which became more defined toward the end of the fifteenth century.

The J. Paul Getty Museum, Los Angeles, California
Unknown craftsman, Carved Walnut Chest, France
Height: 37⅜"; width: 82¼"; depth: 27"

1400s–1500

Early chests were six-plank design—the four sides, a bottom and top. The larger, planked chests were more susceptible to splitting. Frames and panels of Flemish design were far more refined than heavy, planked chests. These Flemish designs provided stress relief from expanding and contracting planks and were more portable because of the lighter-weight construction.

A design detail from the Lowlands was the linenfold motif, usually cut from oak and applied over a walnut panel. This design was cut into the wood using specialty planes much like our molding planes and grooving planes, but these planes were shaped to cut the linenfolds.

The Lowlands' settle was early frame and panel in Gothic motif with closed sides. It served as a bench and a bed, and since it extended to the floor, it was suitable for chest storage under a hinged seat—a deluxe model of the coffer chair.

The Metropolitan Museum of Art, New York City
Unknown craftsman, Settle with Chest Seat, South Lowlands
Height: 54½"; length: 72"; depth: 22¾"
Gift of Mr. and Mrs. Edward Small Moore

1500–1600

The drawer was another innovation from the Lowlands. The drawer was, in fact, probably first a chest within a chest, with drawers in drawer casings appearing soon thereafter. Another good idea in chest making caught on.

The latter half of the sixteenth century spawned the development of drawer chests. Chest-on-drawer and drawers atop front-facing openings—all below a fixed top—which could be used as a bench, a table or a bed became increasingly common. By raising this casework on legs, a dresser (server, sideboard) could be used at table-side to prepare the master's meal.

Small casework chests with drawers or doors were made, but they were nameless until the term "commode" was coined some 100 years later during the Regency period. These small chests were designed to fit against a wall.

Larger chests of drawers followed, but the taking of the chest of drawers to its pinnacle was the creation of the high chest-on-chest that began in England. Though the tallboy originated in England, it became popular and long-lived in America as the highboy.

The coffer chest remained a major piece of furniture in England during the sixteenth century. Raised on legs extending from side panels and sometimes the front, a high degree of chip carving was used to decorate these large boxes.

Probably England, possibly fifteenth century
Carved wood, metal chest
Cooper-Hewett, National Design Museum, Smithsonian Institution/Art Resource, New York
Gift of Harvey Smith, 1968-140-12

1600–1700

During this period, England was creating its Jacobean, Elizabethan, and Carolean designs. In America, the Early Colonial style was predominate.

In Japan, tansu (chests) of the late 1600s were part of the world of shoji (screens) and open dwellings. Palace appointments of sushi cabinets were designed for homes, evolving into tea chests for serving. Coffers and ledger chests kept valuables and budgets. Some larger chests were modular to form steps; these were used for storing clothing and household items.

The tansu in project five (John Gillis) was a product of Far Eastern style and western need. This long end-table chest was designed with a traditional tansu face, complete with hand-forged tansu handles and corner brackets.

In Europe, the coffer chest was out. People preferred casework for drawers and drawer chests. These casework pieces developed into many other cabinet forms.

Europe continued gilding, filigreeing and generally adorning furniture. Not only were the exterior designs highly ornate, chests enclosed elaborate internal configurations of drawers, racks and cubbyholes, which were also tailored to writing desks.

Cabinet on Stand
Probably England, late seventeenth century
Oak, deal, walnut, other woods, bone
Cooper-Hewett, National Design Museum, Smithsonian Institution/Art Resource, New York
Bequest of Mrs. John Innes Kane, 1926-22-43

1700s

This is the period during which the commode was named and made in many forms, including some elaborate bombe casings. These were later equipped with a wash bowl and moved from the parlor to the bedroom.

William and Mary and Queen Anne styles were popularized in America, while overseas the Regency and rococo designs were the ornamentations of the day. The Williamsburg Gentlemen's Tool Chest featured in project eleven is based on English rococo of the 1700s. This style was revived by the craftsmen of colonial Williamsburg and interpreted again in this book by Andrew McPherson.

This 1745 commode is attributed to carver Joachim Dietrich, based on engravings of Francois de Cuvillies. The top is marble, carcass is a carved, gessoed, painted and gilded pine case standing on gilted bronze (ormolu) mounts. Don't try this at home without supervision.

The J. Paul Getty Museum, Los Angeles
Carving attributed to Joachim Dietrich; engravings by Francois de Cuvillies
Commode, about 1745
Carved, painted, and gilded pine; gilt-bronze mounts; jaune rose de Brignolles marble top
Height: 32¾"; width: 49¾"; depth; 24⅜"

Late 1700s

In the mid-eighteenth century the Newport (or Rhode Island) School was building furniture for vacation mansions and exporting its wares to India for English colonizers. This family of furniture builders, Goddard and Townsend of Newport, Rhode Island, built clock cases and high chests with the signature scallop shell decorating the piece.

Hepplewhite (1750–1790) was busy plying his craft as furniture maker. An example in the project section is the Eighteenth Century Federal Sideboard built and decorated with veneers in the Hepplewhite style by Bob Stevenson (project twelve).

Another example of veneering and marquetry is the late eighteenth century Dutch Commode. The example has a top inlaid with satinwood panel and oval medallion of foliage with a geometric border. The front corners are chamfered and inlaid, with inverted obelisk legs following the corner angle. The piece is made from mahogany and stainwood veneer.

Philadelphia Museum of Art
Late eighteenth century Dutch Commode
Bequest of Mrs. C. Emory McMichael

1800–1900

During the Napoleonic Empire period in Europe, furniture in Germany took on the Biedermeier name. Biedermeier is a style of heavy proportions and is highly architectural. In America, John Seymore and Duncan Phyfe were making furniture in the Federal style. Also in America were pockets of emigrated Quakers, well established as Shakers since the last quarter of the 1700s, happily (we think) producing furniture of simple beauty know as Shaker style.

On the simple side as well, the Arts and Crafts movement (around 1875) of William Morris evolved into a more basic design of Craftsman or Mission furniture. The "mission" of Mission furniture was the simplicity of its function.

Shaker furniture was initially for their own use, but they began selling it around 1850. This chest is a good example of their earlier craft.

The Metropolitan Museum of Art, Friends of the American Wing Fund
Shaker, Painted Pine Blanket Chest
Height: 29⅛"; width: 38¾"; depth: 19"

1900s

The efforts of William Morris were being promoted in America through Stickley's publishing and crusading on behalf of the Arts and Crafts mission. These designs were built to look handcrafted and ran counter to ornate styles. The organic furniture of Frank Lloyd Wright's schools of design, Taliesen and Taliesen-West, furthered the marriage of furniture with architecture and reintroduced more fluid, flowing curvatures.

In Europe, pockets of major design forces were maturing. De Stijl (1917) was producing in the Functionalist Modern movement; the Bauhaus (1919) was producing and progressing until Hitler decided it was a threat to the order of supremacy. The Bauhaus was shut down in 1933. Art Deco (1920–1930) focused on rectilinear forms and the use of plastics.

Just look at the time line to see the number of names listed under "Modern." The latter half of the nineteenth century has provided us with numerous names to accompany the variety of styles we see today: names like Maloof, Krenov, Castle, Bennet and Osgood.

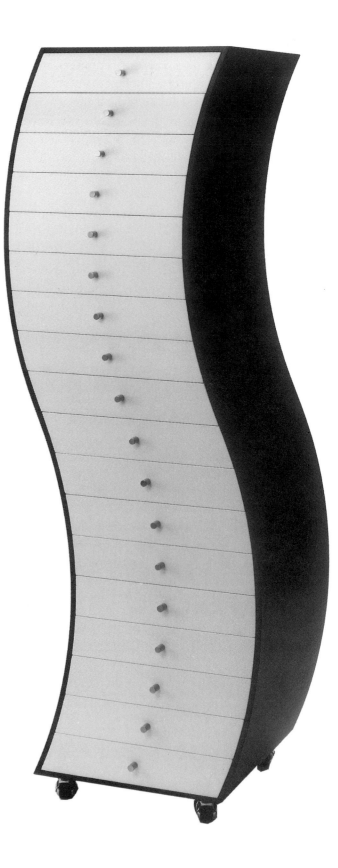

From Furniture in Irregular Forms, a chest from Japanese designer Shiro Kuramata, produced by Italian maker, Cappellini, Arosio, Italy. This irregular chest of drawers is approximately 5½′ in height, and 2′ × 2′ in width and depth. Pieces such as this were typical of the California Design Series of the mid 1970s and continue to show up from the minds and hands of furniture makers.

Philadephia Museum of Art
Designed by Shiro Kuramata, made by Cappellini, Arosio, Italy
Gift of Cappellini, Arosio, Italy, 1970

Nearing the Millennium

Present-day offerings in custom and commercial chest design carry on the lineage of earlier interpretations. The twelve chests showcased in this book represent a small segment of what we build today. Not unlike the Goddard's and Townsend's, the Morris's and Stickley's and contemporary names we read today, woodworkers still summon their skills, knowledge and resources to express their artistic interpretations, in this instance, in chests.

Today's fine furniture galleries showcase some beautiful furniture being produced as one-of-a-kind custom work. Custom productions come from a large variety of sources, like the workshops of Charles Shakleton and, as shown at right, from Doug Green's store, Green's Design Furniture.

This lingerie chest could very well become a museum piece in the year 2100.

Green Design, Portland, Maine
Lingerie Chest, 1998

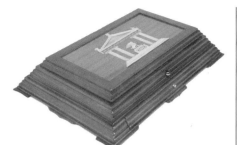

Twelve Chest Projects

STORAGE CHESTS

Deacon's Bench

Rustic Blanket Chest

Spanish Cedar Chest

CHESTS OF DRAWERS

Craftsman Chairside Chest

Japanese Tansu

Shaker Chest of Drawers

Lingerie Chest

SPECIALTY CHESTS

Coin Collector's Chest

Cigar Humidor

Jewelry Chest

Williamsburg Gentleman's
Tool Chest

Eighteenth Century
Federal Sideboard

Deacon's Bench

CAROL REED • RAMONA, CA

> *"It was a learning experience for me, and hopefully it was a learning experience for my class. Those were the two biggest motivations for doing it."*
>
> CAROL REED

Three Views

When invited to participate in this book, Carol was in search of a demonstration project for a woodworking class she was teaching at Palomar College. Satisfying everyone's needs, objectives and schedule, she agreed to build a chest, specifically this modified deacon's bench. She got her demonstration project piece, and we got to follow her design and building processes.

"Modified" is a key word in Carol's deacon's bench discussions. The drawers were included for class demonstration but also added storage beneath the aromatic cedar bottom of the chest lockers. Doors, in this case hinged lids opening to the chest below, demonstrated the steps needed to make doors for furniture.

SPECIFICATIONS

Construction: Frame and panel

Materials: Cherry, cherry and birch veneer plywoods, melamine, aromatic cedar

Height: 30″

Width: 42½″

Depth: 19¾″

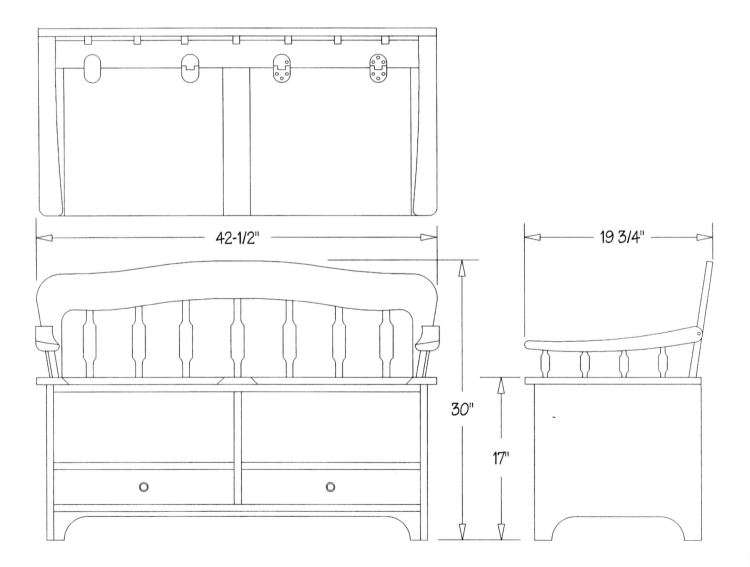

Design Details

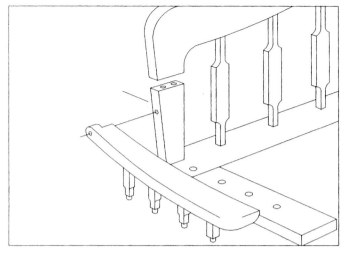

A change in grain orientation from horizontal (the width of the backrest) to vertical grain returning to the bench seat maximizes strength of the back and integrates with the armrest. Arms are dowel pinned and buttoned at the ends and screwed and buttoned from the back.

Drawer materials include a melamine bottom, which is slightly thicker than standard ⅛" increments. "Use one, two or three playing cards to expand a saw dado blade, or to offset the piece for another swipe with the router to net the dado width," Carol told her class. This is when the class suggested the teacher was not playing with a full deck.

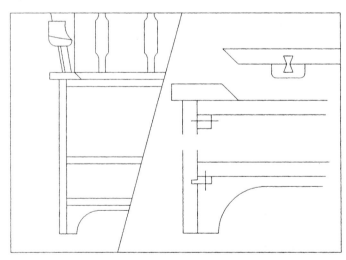

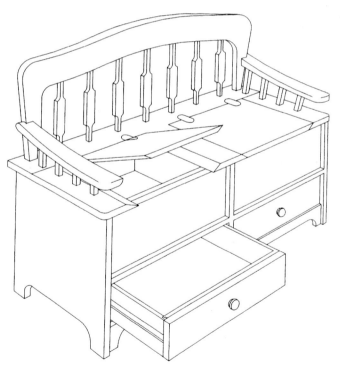

Solid seats are stiffened with a strongback slid onto a cross-grain dovetail rail let into the seat bottoms. The false bottom (of plywood) is fastened with T-clips, allowing sides to slide freely in a dadoed groove, and the top cross-frame cleat is screwed to the solid sides through elongated holes to allow for seasonal expansion and contraction.

Detail of Carol Reed's Deacon's Bench

Work in Progress

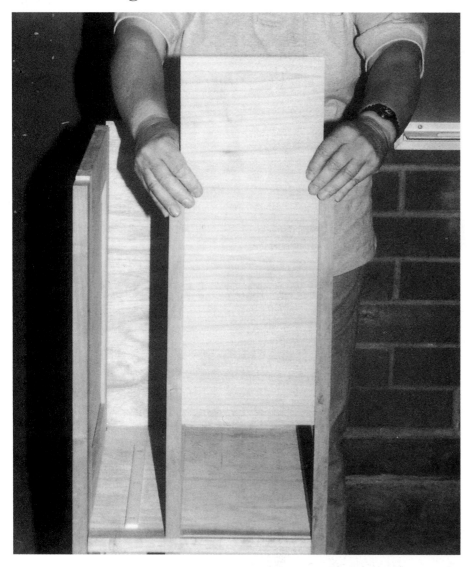

Capturing front veneered plywood panel into dadoed slots. A class discussion ensued on the direction of the vertical grain. The consensus was that the grain should point up to be the most pleasing to the eye.

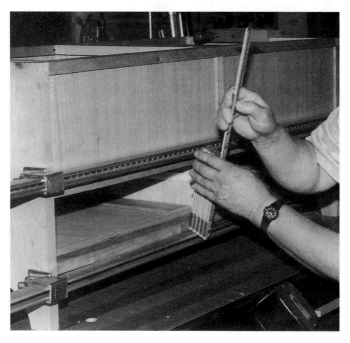

Bringing the glued carcass to "square," Carol made sure the diagonals at the drawer face frame openings are equal. Although dry-fit a few times, this is the moment of truth.

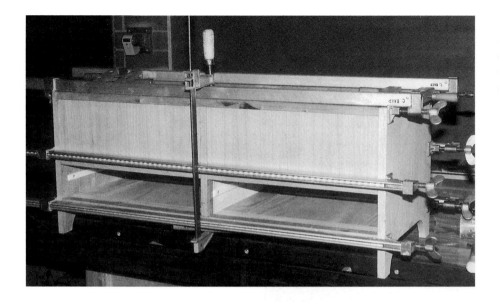

Square-up carcass, amply clamp and allow glue to set. Lightweight aluminum clamps are preferred over heavy pipe clamps because there is less outside stress applied to the clamped piece.

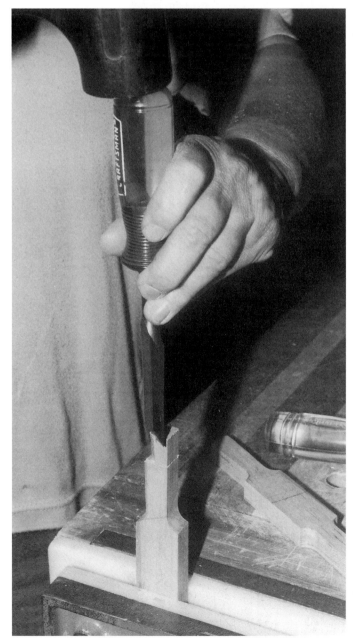

Chamfer the spindle peg to a diameter to be cut by a hollow punch. The ends are first marked with the hole punch, then cut to near round and, finally, shaped by driving the punch home. This saves chucking each up in a lathe.

Drilling 8° holes for arm spindles is made easier by first beveling a board to the desired slant and using it as a drilling fixture when boring holes for the spindle pegs.

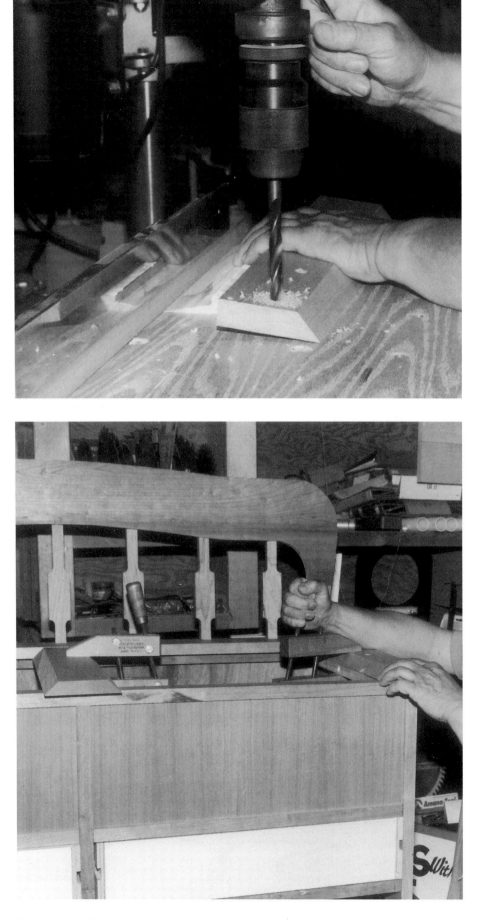

Install pre-drilled bench seat ends, beveled to match and form the 45° seat stops that support the hinged lids.

Variation

This piece could be made as an interpretation in Early American style or as a hybrid of two classic Shaker designs. The thin spindles, associated with a splayed-leg bench, and the heavier chest/bench, which you might find in an early meetinghouse, provide an interesting contrast in weight and proportion. This could be made solid to the floor for maximum storage, but a bootjack at the ends lightens the look.

The Builder's Thoughts

Carol is a professional woodworker specializing in chancel furniture for church congregations throughout the nation. She also creates secular pieces for referral clients. In addition, Carol is president of the San Diego Fine Woodworkers Association, an organization some 1200 members strong. She teaches woodworking in the Cabinet and Furniture Technology program, Palomar College, San Marcos, California.

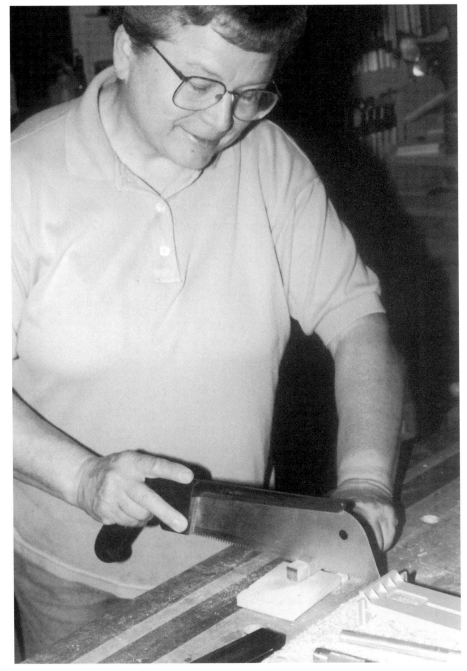

Carol hand cut pegs in the shaped spindles. Starting with a depth cut slightly angled to form the spindle shoulders, she lightly punches the end to mark the diameter in the square. She chisels to a near round and finally lightly drives the hole punch to true the sides.

Questions and Answers

Q Was the design concept in the back of your mind, or did it evolve out of necessity?

A First, I needed to meet some parameters for the class, something that incorporated doors and drawers. And secondly, there were some style things that I wanted to try—a little bit like Sam Maloof in terms of the arms on this piece, a little bit of Arts and Crafts. I was kind of trying to develop a style that I like—a Carol style, as opposed to somebody else's.

Q As you got into the design, even early at the computer, were your ideas altered in the design process or during construction?

A Always. Actually, I'm pretty good at designing on the computer and having the piece come out fairly close. There were a few things that I had to incorporate as I was building it that didn't occur to me as I was drawing it—like my choice to use solid wood at the sides. I had to account for a little more than $\frac{1}{4}''$ of expansion/contraction over the 16″ panel. There was that issue. Then there were the seats themselves, which are the lids for the chest under the seats. They are also solid wood, so I dovetailed a pair of battens cross-grain near each end of the lids to keep them flat. That was an added change, but that's the nature of dealing with solid woods and not really thinking that part through in the initial design.

Q So the grain runs in which direction?

A Grain runs the width of the piece. They were glued up from solid wood and cut in two so the grain matches from one lid to the other. I also had another opportunity to match grain across the two drawer fronts—that's a single piece of wood cut into two pieces. I managed to keep the grain going, which adds to the custom look.

Q So the dovetail runs? . . .

A From front to back. Actually from the back to almost the front. It doesn't come out the front. I did dovetail a batten in there one-third of the way in. It also stands proud from the bottom of the seat, so it is also aesthetic. It's all rounded off. You can't tell they're dovetails. You would have to take the lid off and look behind the hinge at the back.

Q What is the drawer design detail?

A They have a melamine bottom, which is very nice because they need no drawer liners. The drawer sides are

made of $\frac{1}{2}''$ birch ply. Dimensionally stable. Nice stuff to work with. Corners are joined with a locking rabbet. The ends of the drawer front and back get the rabbet; the sides get the dadoes. I added on a false front and maintained the grain pattern.

Q If you were to do a second one now, how would you approach it differently?

A I would do the arms differently, but I'm not exactly sure how. The shape of the arms are reminiscent of the Maloof rocker. I like that sculptured look, and that was kind of fun to do. I had problems fitting the spindles. I think I drilled the holes prematurely. Fitting top and bottom at the same time, I got some wild angles. It made fitting a whole lot more difficult than it needed to be. Before I did it again, I would do some serious study on what other chair makers had done in terms of building something with spindle backs, spindles under the arms. I just kind of winged my way through it without doing some serious study.

Q You mentioned this was your first seat. Style-wise was it altogether different from anything you had done?

A Yes. I don't normally build out of that much solid wood. Actually there were two things that played into that. One, I wanted to show my class the care that one needed to take and the planning that one had to do when building with that much solid wood. Secondly, I was challenged by seeing some of Maloof's furniture and thought I should try it.

I now think building something with a back on it and with arms may not be anything I ever do again. It certainly reinforced my decision to not build seating as a profession. It takes far too long. It's more a labor of love and does not even come close to being remotely profitable. But I had an opportunity to work with more solid woods, and I had the cherry in the shop, so I didn't have to buy a whole lot of wood. That was a consideration also because this was a piece for myself, or maybe a piece on spec, which I never do, and I didn't want to put a whole lot of money into it. I think I have a pretty challenging piece and potentially a valuable piece without having a whole lot of cash in it.

Q You mention Maloof. Is there a particular style or woodworker that you lean toward?

A I try not to emulate someone else's style. At least not in the whole. The only woodworker's style that motivates me at all is Sam Maloof's. I had the pleasure of meeting the guy a couple of times, saw his shop, met his wife, been in his house. Just being around him, listening to him talk about woodworking, is probably the single most motivating factor to make you come home and get into the shop. He is so talented. He is such an easy-going guy, and he makes it seem so simple that you really want to get out there and try it.

He was a graphic artist, a graphic designer before he became a woodworker. He became a woodworker after he got married and didn't have any money for furniture, so he started building furniture. But he violates all straight-line rules that most woodworkers seem to think that wood has to be built with. Sam makes it do curves. He alludes the eye. He makes the eye go somewhere where you don't expect the eye to go. His pieces are interesting. They have a certain style and flair to them that makes them very comfortable, and in addition to that, they *are* comfortable. He makes you want to try things that are outside the norm.

Q In your designs for commercial customers, not for the chancel furniture, do you design primarily for function or the art form?
A Function. I see myself as a problem-solver as opposed to an artist. I try to make things look aesthetically pleasing. I keep looking for opportunities to exercise that side of my brain. My first goal is to solve a problem with that piece of furniture—it's going to have to do something, it has to serve a function. I try to make it serve its function uniquely and be aesthetically pleasing. But first, function.

Q Any new methods used in joiner work or materials?
A Not really. I guess the only different thing I did do was make the round tenons on the ends of the spindles with a metal punch. That's the first time I'd ever tried that. It worked pretty well. It got them the right diameter

and did a pretty good job of getting them straight. That was an example of misusing a tool, but it served a function and it worked well.

Q Do you have a favorite tool?
A I was able to get rid of my old chop saw and my radial arm saw when I bought my compound miter saw.

Q Any message or tip to help out and get a woodworker started to build a piece like the bench or on woodworking in general?
A What I tell my students is that, as far as I am concerned, furniture building should follow some rules. The first one is to determine the need—what purpose the piece should fill. Until you have a clear idea of that, you don't really have any idea what it is you're building. And once you have determined the function that piece is going to serve, then you can start taking a look at style and features, gathering information from other sources, throwing out what doesn't fit or what you don't like, and leaving in what you do.

I would encourage people to reach a little. Attempt a design of their own. Don't just go with somebody else's design. Be creative. Put your individualism into the piece. Wing it and see what happens. What is the worst thing that could happen? You wind up with an expensive door-stop or a candidate for the fireplace. I really doubt that. There is so much self-satisfaction that comes out of designing your own piece in that you've designed it logically, you've decided what it should be. Here it needed to be a bench, but it also needed to have doors and drawers and serve its function as a chest, a take-off on a deacon's bench, which was a chest. It just kind of evolved. I think I would like to encourage letting those ideas evolve and build a piece out of those ideas, rather than off some piece of paper.

Rustic Blanket Chest

MARTIN PREVOSTO • IDYLLWILD, CA

"... as you're milling, the first look is exciting—you can see the colors that come out in the wood and kind of figure out what you will make out of it. I think it's more rewarding—you're more involved."

MARTIN PREVOSTO

Three Views

The Prevostos arrived in Idyllwild in 1991, contracted to build a mountain cabin. The building permit had a proviso (a Prevosto's Proviso?) that trees cleared from the cabin site would be used in its construction. This launched his interest in slab-milling his own lumber and in a line of furniture with "The Natural Edge."

Rustic furniture is made in a variety of ways, including stick, willow, slab, and in styles ranging from country to contemporary. The example in this book is a favorite for cabin furniture in the mountains, or in a hideaway room of a suburban home.

SPECIFICATIONS

Construction: Slab

Materials: Local Jeffery pine, aromatic cedar lining

Height: 22″

Width: 50″

Depth: 21½″

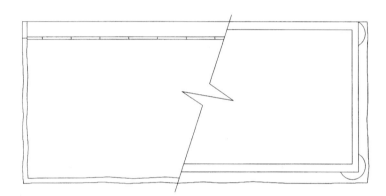

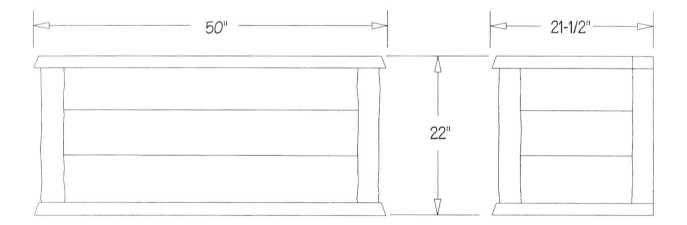

Design Details

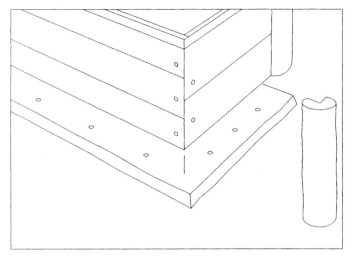

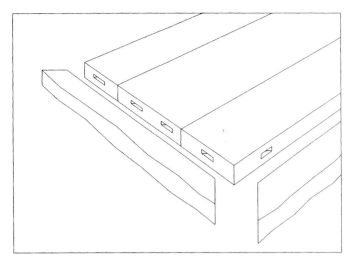

In building heavy slab furniture, lag bolts are more in scale with the measure than dowels, so some of the joinery includes gluing and bolting the slabs in place. For this design, wood screws countersunk from the underside were adequate.

Rejoining a natural edge may not seem too natural, but nature didn't know the dimensions of the final piece. The chest top, for example, was butt joined to form the panels. The natural edge was rejoined to the sides—a necessary step if covering the end grain. Marty snaps a chalk line about 2″ in from the edge, then rips the edge using a circular saw. A pass or two over the jointer plane brings the edge opposite the natural edge true for gluing.

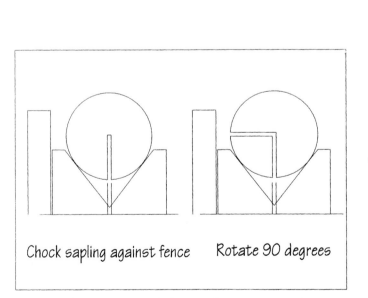

Chock sapling against fence   Rotate 90 degrees

Corner saplings present a challenge when cutting a 90° cutout to snug against a corner. Many saplings are straight enough to rip away the quarter section against the guide fence; others may need chocking in a v-block to feed and cut true.

Rustic Blanket Chest

Work in Progress

Jeffery, ponderosa and sugar pines and cedar are selectively logged from local, privately-owned land. These trees are most likely diseased or damaged, posing a potential hazard for the owner and some interesting wood grain, texture and color for the furniture builder. They may be donated outright, or Marty may have to pay a logger to remove and deliver in specified lengths for slabbing. He then mills the lumber using an Alaskan Mill.

"Where we are, we don't have a kiln or shed—we wrap everything in plastic and let it air-dry. Usually three to four months per inch is enough because it is so dry up here. We keep everything covered and stickered and the ends painted to keep them dry. Summer heat is bad. You really have to watch it because it tends to take off on you. Drying too fast, it can warp and check if you're not paying attention."

"The jointer and thickness planer are run every day. And anything wider than my surface planer can handle is taken to a wide-belt sander in Huntington Beach where we can run up to 51″-widths. The widest I have now is 48″, and that's a big tree."

Biscuits, bought in bulk, are used to edge-glue slabs to width. A heavy-duty biscuit joiner speeds production. Biscuits are quick and easy—not nearly as demanding as aligning dowels and just as strong.

Freshly milled, air-dried wood exposed to oxygen can develop a variety of colors caused by fungus in the wet sapwood. Controlled drying conditions of a kiln or in a forced-air shed can reduce or eliminate discoloration. Slabs that were stacked on edge before being stickered begin to develop areas of blue stain. This coloration, along with the natural edge, adds to the uniqueness of the piece.

Variations

Slab construction can easily be adapted to common lumber thicknesses. To combine Marty's proposed drawer arrangement (which the client didn't want) with the approach Carol Reed took on the Deacon's Bench (project one), adding drawers to a rustic or a more refined shell, is readily do-able.

This page of variations includes modifying Marty's design as shown at left and right below, and a look at a simple Shaker chest (bottom), inspired by the real thing pictured in the time line (page 21).

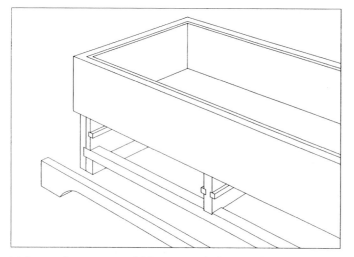

Make two bottoms or add bearing rails front and back below a false bottom to form the drawer casings.

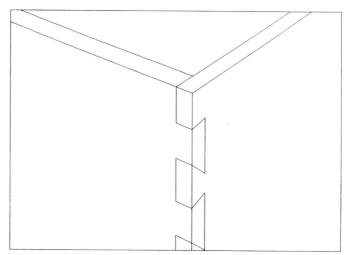

The rustic chest look, with or without drawers, could include some large dovetails or heavy-duty box joints at the corners.

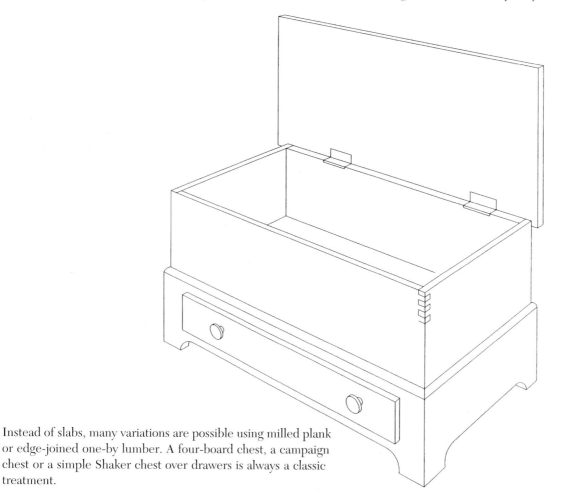

Instead of slabs, many variations are possible using milled plank or edge-joined one-by lumber. A four-board chest, a campaign chest or a simple Shaker chest over drawers is always a classic treatment.

The Builders' Thoughts

Edye, Marty's partner, spouse and accountant, also embarks (sorry) on the task of stripping bark from saplings and slabs. Bark is removed back to the cambium layer, leaving the random coloring and shape of the natural edge.

Marty Prevosto sets up his milling operation on his property in a stand of pine trees—not a bad place to work.

Questions and Answers

Q What are your thoughts on sharing your project with other woodworkers?
A I think it's great. A lot of people have questions and maybe I can give some answers. It's fun to help people who are trying to get where they want to go in woodworking. Unless you go to school there aren't too many places to learn from different people—to show you what they know.

Q You mentioned your interest in boats—growing up around the Chesapeake, then going to California as a ship's carpenter. How did you get into building rustic furniture?
A While working as a boat carpenter, I heard about a small start-up company making furniture, and I've always had an interest in that aspect of the trade. I really enjoy it. I think it is more rewarding to build furniture than anything else. You just get more out of it. People enjoy what you make and express their pleasure when they find a piece, or have a piece made for them.

Q What were your objectives for this blanket chest?
A Basically I got measurements from the client. She wanted it a certain size for the things she wanted to store. I drew it up from her specifications.

Q Had she bought from you earlier?
A No. But she had seen our stuff, and we showed her photos of things we have made, and she said she would like us to make a blanket chest for her, so we went from there.

Q Any changes to the initial design concept, your initial thoughts?
A It was pretty much built as proposed. I suggested drawers across the bottom, but she didn't want a drawer. It is basically a box with a lid.

Q The cedar lining was her request?
A Yes. She wanted aromatic cedar, so she got what she wanted.

Q Were these ideas altered during construction?
A No, but I could have gotten a little fancier, maybe interlocking joints on the corners, not like a dovetail, but like large finger joints. And maybe I could have added a sliding tray.

Q Any major challenges in construction, materials, finish?
A The hardest thing is keeping all the materials flat when you are doing the milling by yourself. The thinner you mill, the harder it is to keep it from twisting. I just kept stuff piled up on it to keep the weight on it. If you can keep it flat, you can make anything.

Q The lid thickness is 1¾", and the sides? . . .
A They wound up being 1". I milled them 1¼", which is as thin as I can go on the mill using the chainsaw. I was milling everything 1¾", but had to go to 2" because that extra ¼" puts more weight on and keeps stuff from twisting. So I mill 2" and 1¼", and the 1¼" is usually re-milled to 1" on a wide-belt sander or run through the surface planer.

Q The "Natural Edge" style has become your business trademark. It started with building a cabin in Idyllwild, and you were required to use the trees cleared from the building site?

A We had to cut down 13 trees for the new house to go up, and in doing that the people said we needed to use this lumber some way, so I figured out how I could mill it for cabinets, paneling and all the door casings. Countertops were also made from trees on the property.

Q Were those ponderosa . . . Jeffery pine?
A They were all Jefferies, except for one. We had one good sized incense cedar about 30″ across the bottom. We used the cedar for the kitchen countertop and the bathroom. Everything else was from the pine.

Q What would you do differently in a second item?
A I suggested a pair of drawers across the bottom, but the client opted for more inside space. Another requested design feature was to keep the chest hard against a wall, so the top was ripped and the hinge inset from the back so the hinged lid stays open a little beyond the vertical.

Q You've built both fine and rustic furniture. Were you influenced by a particular style, era or woodworker?
A I prefer the rustic because you can leave it natural, the way the tree grew—especially the edges. I worked many years doing antique reproductions in oak, and you can make only so much of it, because you see so much of it. I think the pine furniture is really refreshing. It is cleaner. I don't recommend staining it, but if you leave it natural with a clear finish, the colors come out over time. It's just pretty.

Q How much attention do you pay to function over appearance?
A Basically everything I build is to a standard height. I have a book of furniture standards—heights for coffee tables, dining room tables, desks, even how to figure space for each person at a round table. I design basically on that, keeping a standard height, and design the depth and width for its location—where the piece of furniture has to fit.

Q Any new methods used in joiner work, materials, finishes?
A It's pretty basic. No fancy joints. Probably the fanciest would be a mortise and tenon, or a blind mortise. No dovetailing. Using the biscuit cutter for joints adds a lot of strength to a butt joint.

Q What is your favorite, or the most frequently used, tool in the shop?
A Probably the jointer and thickness planer. Those machines are run every day. And anything wider than my surface planer can handle is taken to a wide-belt sander in Huntington Beach where we can run up to 51″-wide slabs. The widest I have now is 48″.

Q You mentioned a special chainsaw blade for your Alaskan Mill?
A I am using a full-competition blade with a chisel cut on the Alaskan Mill. That's pretty aggressive, but I found that works the best for what we're milling. I can mill up to 40 slabs from one chain without resharpening, thanks to the chromium steel used in this particular chain. With all the other chains I can probably cut 15 slabs and that's it. Then it gets dull and I have to put on another chain.

Q What about a Wood-Mizer. Can you use it up here?
A I have access to a Wood-Mizer, but it's limited to only 26″, where I can cut to 49″ with the Alaskan Mill, and it's more portable and versatile. I can throw it in the back of the truck whenever I need to mill at the site, whereas a Wood-Mizer is on a trailer, and lifting the logs to the mill table requires another piece of equipment. With the Alaskan Mill, the log can be on the ground as I work.

Q You seem to enjoy the milling as much as building the furniture.
A It goes hand in hand. In doing your own milling, you can see the process it takes to make lumber. I think it's more rewarding when you see a log or tree that has been cut down, then you cut it up and mill it, and as you're milling, you can see all the colors that come out in the wood and you can say well I can make this out of that piece. You can kind of figure out what you're going to make out of it as you mill the log. I think it is more rewarding . . . you're more involved.

Q What message would you give the readers who want to do rustic slab work?
A If they want to mill, become knowledgeable about chainsaws and how to use them. Also they should learn the whole milling process—setting up to mill a log, and the techniques of milling, stickering and air-drying, which are really important. You can mill a log, and if it's not stickered right, you could lose your lumber and all that work would be for nothing.

Spanish Cedar Chest

GARTH GRAVES • SAN DIEGO, CA

> "Designed and built for the ladies in my life, three blanket chests are unique, tailored to their tastes (I hope) and to their surroundings."
>
> GARTH GRAVES

Three Views

There isn't any Spanish cedar (Central American species of the mahogany family) in this Spanish Cedar Chest, but "Aromatic Cedar-Lined, Spanish-Style Blanket Chest" is too long for a project title. A "cedar" chest may be more definitively named a hope, dowry, blanket or marriage chest, depending on its origin and your roots.

SPECIFICATIONS

Construction: Frame and panel carcass

Materials: White oak, aromatic cedar lined

Height: 22¼"

Width: 35½"

Depth: 19¾"

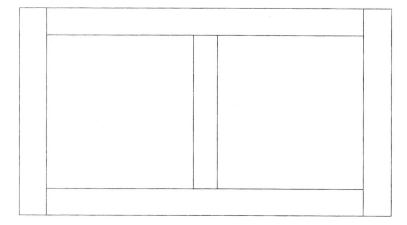

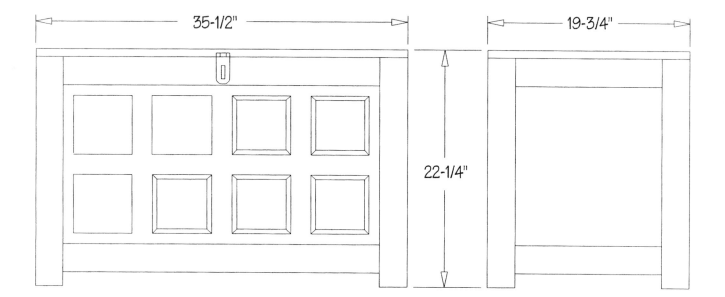

Design Details

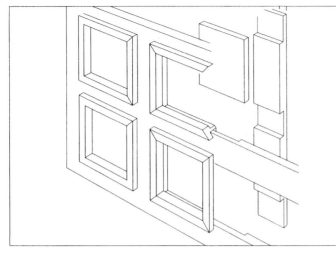

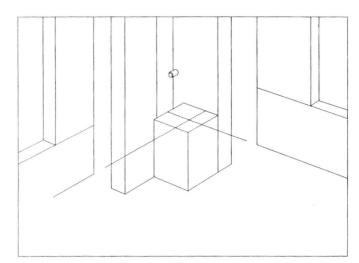

Cut-away view of molding profile offers one idea for varying the relief. Panels can stand proud of the frame, flush with the frame or inset. Cedar lining covers these panels at the backside, eliminating the need for a finished back, but keep the back of these panels flush or inset.

Corner posts are build-ups of right-angled corners for attaching panels, and extend to form the short legs. The post's face is full-width, joined 90° with a narrower piece butted, doweled and glued to form a corner of equal sides. The extended leg is filled with an oak block to complete the four sides of the post. Joinery could be a stopped lapped butt joint or a rabbeted slot joint.

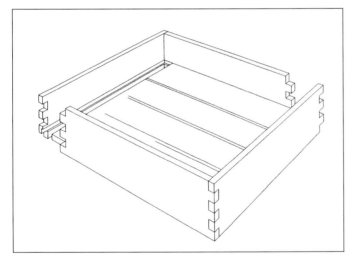

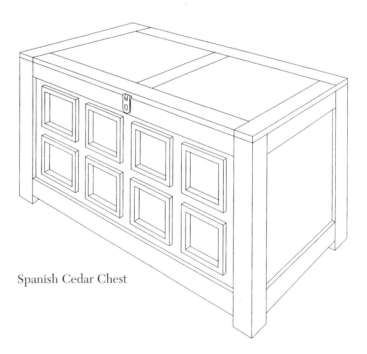

The sliding tray is made from tongue and groove cedar as well. Tray bottom is a build-up using the tongue and groove joints, but could be trimmed and butt glued to form a solid bottom. Sides are full width boards, less the tongue and groove edge. Corners are finger joined and the bottom lets into a dado inside the tray.

Spanish Cedar Chest

Work in Progress

A simple spacing jig for the table or radial-arm saw steps off dado locations for half-lapped joints. Use a hollow-ground blade for clean facing edges, and a piece of scrap block behind the cut to prevent blow-out. A cleaner cut may result if you route these dado joints on a shaper, router table or portable router.

With all pieces cut to size and dry fit to ensure all is proper, glue up assembly, keeping all members flat and square. Glue alone should hold the half-lap junctions, but a short counter-sunk screw in from the backside would provide added insurance. Whether screwed or not, clamp these junctions while the glue sets.

Install molding around opening to capture the panels between the vertical and horizontal half-lapped stringers (stiles and rails). Attach molding around the opening, then insert and attach the subpanels inside each frame.

Installing built-up panels with top and bottom rails attached is best done between assembled ends, keeping the shell square and true. Once the four sides are glued and screwed in place, the protruding legs can be filled with a block to form the other two sides of the post, which also supports the side panels and chest bottom.

Slide top panels into place. The top panels of white oak-veneered ⅜" plywood (also used for the sides and bottom) were rabbeted to slide into the top frame. The bottom was screwed and glued to cleats, which in turn were screwed and glued around the apron.

Cut finger joints in sliding cedar tray. Using another jig clamped to the miter guide, the fingers and spaces of equal width are dadoed into the tray sides. This is a good opportunity to add dovetails for decoration, in addition to adding the monogram chip carved into the tray back. The tray rests on cedar slide cleats with rounded-over edges glued and tacked onto the cedar lining.

Variations

Whether, or even if, you divide the panel sides is open to your choice. Of foremost importance is meeting your design objective for the piece, to match or contrast with future surroundings. Make this an opportunity to produce a style you've been waiting to try.

All panels may be left plain for a more contemporary look, the simple side of the design scale, or they may be divided into vertical panels for an English or Flemish feel. Styles at the opposite end of the design spectrum might be divided further, still in the Mexican or Spanish motif.

There are a whole slew of design possibilities by simplifying or adding yet more ornamentation.

Approach the construction as with any frame and panel project, adding to or reducing the relief by applying molding standing proud of the frame, or adding a raised center to the inset panel, or further indenting the panel inside the frame. However, too many small shapes and planes may be too much for the look and for the effort.

You could add drawers across the bottom, producing a chest-over-drawer hope, dowry or blanket chest.

Plain, solid (or plywood) panels are candidates for a simple decorative detail as a focal point.

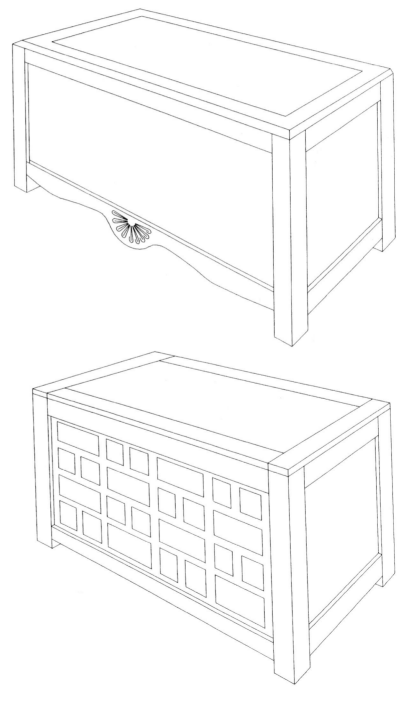

Or the frames can be divided into more panels (smaller openings) by reducing the width of the rails and stiles. The variation shown divides larger squares into two rectangles, and one of those rectangles into two square panels. These three-panel squares can be alternated or rotated to vary the pattern.

The Builder's Thoughts

I invited myself to build a chest for the book with the objective of filling any gaps in the array of designs, and maybe adding some personal contribution and interpretation. The foremost objective was to present as a collection a variety of chest styles approached from individual perspectives, showcasing a broad range of results.

The author dadoes a rabbet along the stile to let in the paneled frame at the corner.

Questions and Answers

Q What were the objectives for this project?
A I decided to build three blanket chests for the three ladies in my life (plus an oak computer desk for my son so he wouldn't feel slighted). For myself? To get the book done and to the publisher.

Q What sparked the interest, this willingness to be included?
A It's my project. I couldn't refuse.

Q Did you make any alterations during construction?
A Each lady had a different need, a different decor, so I altered the design in each, but kept with the frame and panel method throughout, although the two versions not included in this book were simpler in detail and design.

Q Were there any challenges in construction?
A I had worked with the Spanish motif in the past, building cupboards and furniture using the framed panel of various combinations in both elevation and profile, so it was just more of the same.

Q What might have been done differently?
A The largest blanket chest has some fairly long panels between narrower corner brackets. Where the chest is located now, the floor slopes and the chest needs to be

shimmed to eliminate the twist. I should have beefed up the corners, or made a separate base and let in the sides, or added a cross-braced bottom to reduce or eliminate the twist.

Q Was the design similar to the present style?
A I try to build things that will fit into the environment. In our home of mixed everything, that isn't difficult. I guess I am perpetuating that mix by building in all styles, but nothing ultra-traditional or ultra-modern. I like clean lines, almost rectilinear in design, and lean toward that type of furniture.

Q Is the design influenced by any particular style or era?
A I go through phases. Early work from the 1960s was Danish influenced. During the 1970s this gave way to Spanish (living in San Diego by way of the Southwest), and today my appreciation of Mission, Stickley and Craftsman is growing. I guess I go with the flow.

Q Are designs primarily functional or an art form?
A They verge on spartan, very utilitarian. Whatever art is there would hopefully be the interpretation of the total piece—balance, symmetry, shape, proportion and composition.

Craftsman Chairside Chest

GARTH GRAVES • SAN DIEGO, CA

> *"I approached this chest based on what Greene and Greene might have produced if commissioned to design a four-square, four-drawer chairside chest of drawers."*
>
> GARTH GRAVES

Three Views

The height of this Craftsman-style chairside chest was designed by Ford engineers. A Ford Explorer pulled onto and over a clamped side panel which had been left gluing on the floor of my garage/workshop. It flattened the corner of one post, so the design height of 23″ became 22″.

I guess the drawer size decision can be attributed elsewhere as well. The carcass was designed to fit four drawer faces I could get out of a length of cherry at its milled width. The project was built backwards—the drawers were made first, then the case designed to house them.

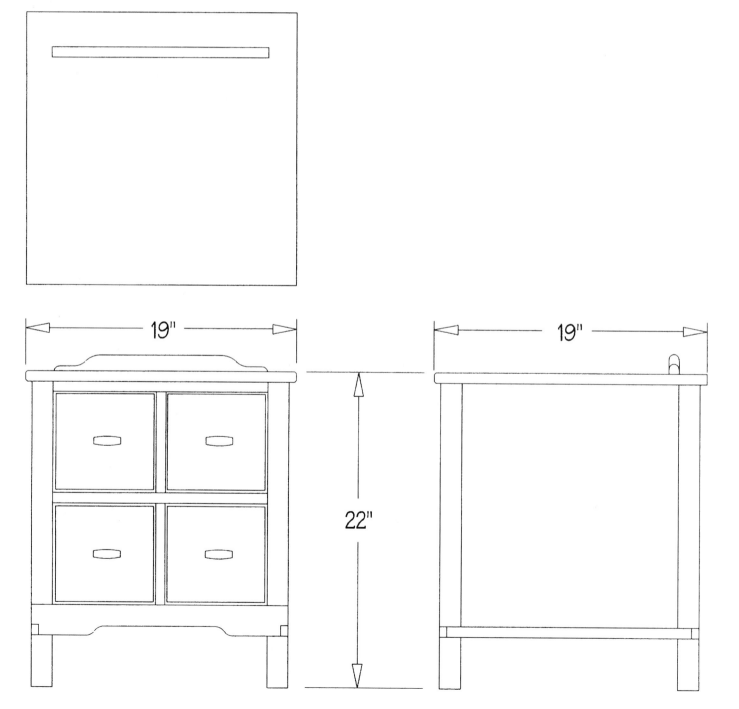

Design Details

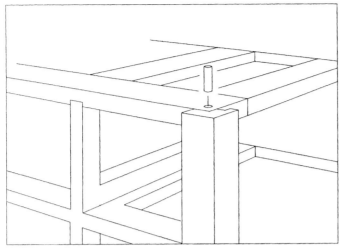

The top frame, let into the corner posts, is doweled at a slight angle into posts to prevent pull-out. With a little forethought, the upper bearing rail could have been cut longer and dovetailed into the top ends of the flanking 2″ × 2″ legs.

Drawer bearer frames form the armature for this carcass. Corner posts (this time really posts) were relieved to receive the lower and middle drawer bearer frame.

This stepped, half-lapped rail, designed earlier on a small computer desk, steps at the intersecting side rails which lap both vertically and horizontally at the face. These were doweled from behind, but an exposed pin or plug covering a slotted screw would be true to the style and add another design element.

The top is attached with screws in slotted holes cut through the upper bearing frame for swelling and shrinking of the top and sides across the grain.

Work in Progress

Routing dovetails in drawer sides using a guide produces less of a custom look but is an attractive joint just the same. Some schools of thought would have you shy away from using different woods for the drawer face and sides, but having experienced no problem with different rates of expansion and contraction, I use contrasting woods to accentuate the dovetails.

Round over the edges on the drawer sides. This could have been done quicker and cleaner using a router, but that was set up to do dovetails, so the drill press served as a shaper table in a pinch. A tapered spindle holds the Jacob's chuck firmly during side loads of a shaper bit.

Dry fitting drawer parts reduces, and hopefully eliminates, surprises when glued for good. A drawer bottom is let in around all four sides, and the last installed side piece captures the bottom.

The bearing frames begin with ripping 1″ cherry wide enough to serve as drawer runners. A dado is cut down the inside edge of the front and the back to receive a matching tongue cut into the three lengths that will form the sides and center divider.

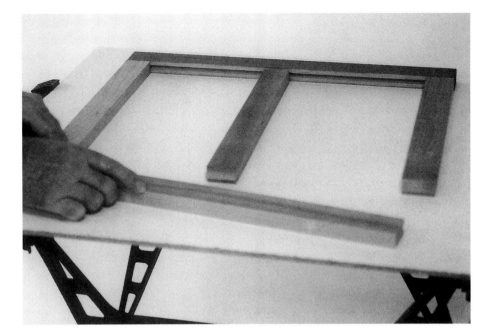

A wide groove was dadoed into the glued-up frames to receive the thickness of the center stiles, aligned above and below the center rail forming the four-drawer casings. The front facing edges of the bearers were grooved to receive a tongued facing. I wasn't sure how much to inset the drawers from the 2″ × 2″ posts. This practice would also be used if a different material was used for the substructure frames.

After squaring up the boards that make up the sides and top and planing the joining edges, the dowel location was marked in facing boards and drilled laterally on the Shopsmith. This aligned the dowel holes the same distance from the top surfaces when placed face down on the saw table.

Variations

This classic four-drawer design could be scaled up or down with extended or no legs (to set on a tabletop or counter) for the kitchen, pantry or great room. Pine would be a good wood of choice, as would oak or whatever complements the look you want to achieve.

The casework also lends itself to an open shell by re-moving the drawer casing frames and adding a drop-front desk panel, and maybe an organizer of small drawers, slots and pigeonholes. This could be a tabletop chest, corners could be extended as legs or a separate stand could be built for this Spanish Vargueño.

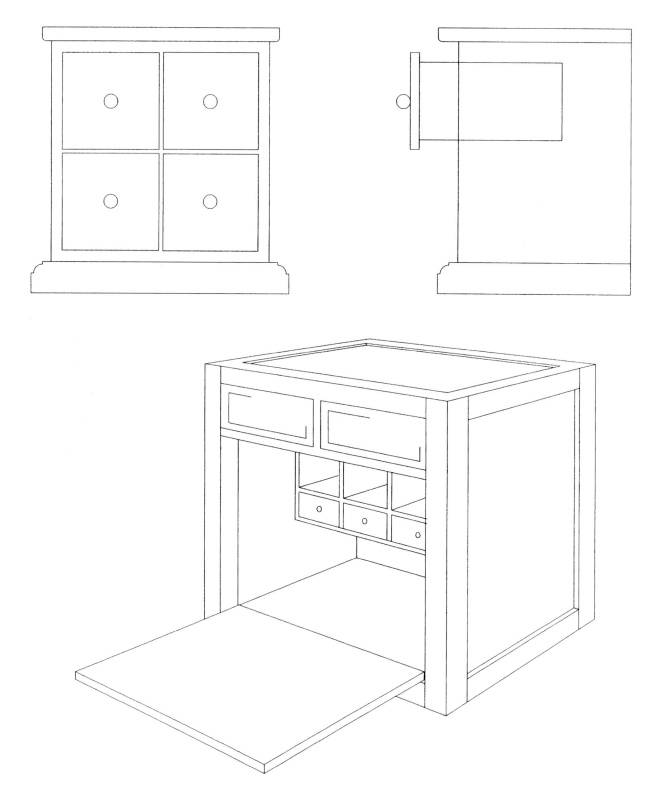

The Builder's Thoughts

Six of the twelve chests featured here were entries in the San Diego Fine Woodworking's Design in Wood show (and two others were built by principals in that show), so the timing for this book was right to catch furniture builders preparing their wooden chests.

A woodworker for more than 35 years, Garth Graves has gained a lot of insight into furniture design and construction. His knowledge of ancient and modern furniture-making has not only helped him with his own woodworking, but it has also helped other woodworkers through his book *The Woodworker's Guide to Furniture Design*, as well as through many other books and articles.

Questions and Answers

Q What was the initial design concept for your second project for this book?

A I wondered what Greene and Greene might have produced if commissioned to design a four-square, four-drawer chairside chest of drawers.

Q Were these ideas altered during construction?

A I took certain liberties with their "signature" through-mortise tenons by designing a half-lap apron stepped under the drawer face and along the lower panel line.

Q Any major challenges in construction, materials, finish?

A It was built backwards, beginning with drawers because I had a piece of cherry calling out to be drawer faces, followed by an armature of frames (top, drawer bearers and verticals), then the side and back panels. Using Stan Piechota's approach (described later in project seven) for the drawer-bearing rails, I built full riding surfaces for the drawers let into the sides rather than attaching drawer guides and cleats individually to the inside of the shell.

Q What could be done differently in a second item?

A I would probably inset the sides from the legs for a simpler rabbet, and look seriously at ⅜″ or ½″ cherry veneer plywood for the sides rather than dadoes and rabbets to let in the ¾″ thickness to the legs, and not have to relieve the sides and back to clear the bearing-rail frames.

Q Was it a departure? And if so, why?

A I'll forego my rectilinear spiel, and just say for this piece I wanted something fairly complex, yet simple, and on the small side for some future apartment abode.

Q What influenced this piece?

A I like the simple lines of Craftsman style, especially contemporary adaptations. I use past examples for inspiration, but like to add my own interpretation.

Q Any new methods used in joinery, materials, finishes for this second project?

A I adopted (stole) the bearing rail/frame approach used in the lingerie chest (project seven). And for the first time in all these years, I set up the Shopsmith to dress-sand the panels (instead of taking these panels to the wide-belt sanding store).

Q In this self-interview, should I be exempt from offering a tip to the reader?

A I guess not. My philosophy, and some might call it a crusade, dates back to 1970s magazine articles containing not only how-to, but you-can messages—encouraging woodworkers of all skill levels to extend their horizons of design and workmanship. You grow with each new project. It just happens. And it happens without my, or anyone else's, advice, but if that process can be accelerated through a little encouragement, so much the better.

Japanese Tansu

E. JOHN GILLIS • YUCAIPA, CA

> *"I usually don't have to draw something more than twice. Usually in the first drawing I can spot things I might have done wrong."*
>
> JOHN GILLIS

Three Views

For this project much of the design work was done for John. The client presented a photo of the desired tansu, and John worked it from there. As an avid collector of antique tools, and antique planes in particular, John uses his collected assortment when building in his period furniture style. He is especially proud of a few unused planes dating back to the early 1800s. One has a blade that cuts a double ogee reverse with three beads.

SPECIFICATIONS

Construction: Edge-glued panels, dovetailed carcass

Materials: Ash with golden color finish

Height: 22″

Width: 17″

Depth: 32″

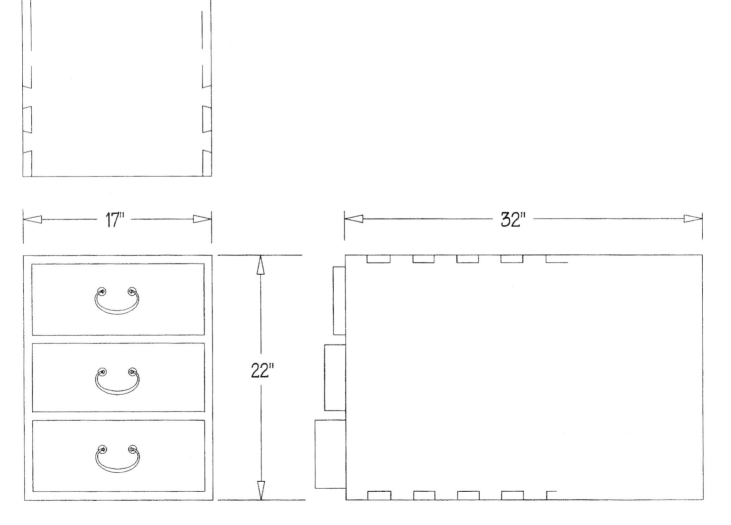

Design Details

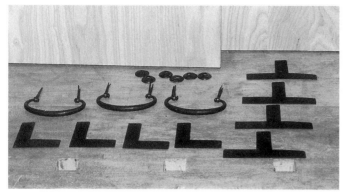

Tansu hardware is a distinctive feature of tansu furniture style, available from The Japan Woodworker, Alameda, California, and Musigi Design in Berkeley, California.

Plane a rabbet for the rear panel enclosing the four-sided case. Finally, an application for one of his antique rabbeting planes.

Carcass shell ready for drawer runners and bearer rails shows the simplicity of this construction. Large dovetails joining the carcass panels create a strong shell. The back panel and drawer-bearing rails add to the rigid construction.

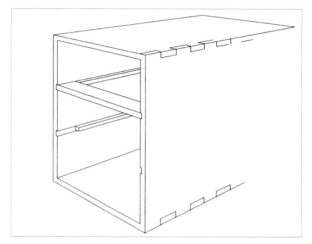

Drawer runners are 1″ × 2″ ash fastened into ¾″ grooves dadoed the depth of the cabinet. Runners will be glued for the first 12″ in from the front, and the remainder will be screwed in place (through generous relief slots) into the carcass for weather-related expansion and contraction across the grain. With the 32″ sides, the ½ percent (or ¼″ per foot) change in size would result in a dimension change of ⅓″. This could cause separation or splitting if fastened securely end-to-end.

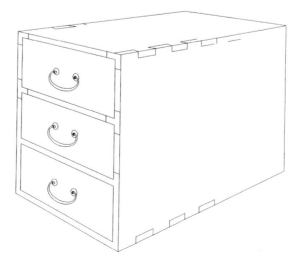

Work in Progress

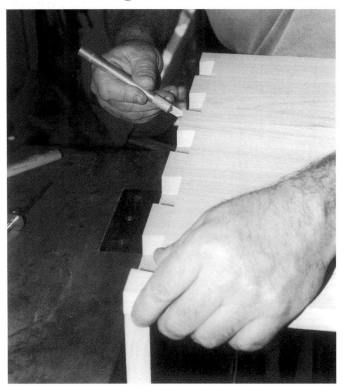

Scribe the dovetail location. The mating dovetail pattern for the adjoining piece is scribed with a stylus.

Hand-cut dovetails are all made to the same depth thanks to the spine on the razor-back saw being exactly ⅛″ above the sawtooth, thus creating a built-in depth gauge. John uses a level—doesn't trust his eye—to square up the piece to be cut, and marks a few reference pencil lines perpendicular to the edge to keep his cuts straight.

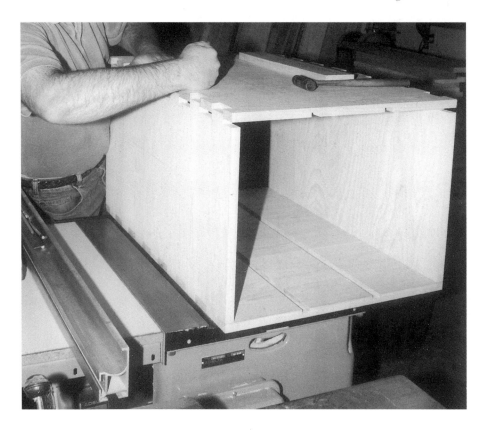

Dry fitting dovetailed corners of this four-panel carcass will indicate interference from the dovetails. Cuts are made to the outside edge of the scribed line, so any fitting is a matter of trimming away.

Drawer joinery is comprised of half-blind dovetails joining the sides to face.

Through dovetails extending beyond the drawer back serve as a stop. These can be trimmed to fit if necessary.

This is the finished tansu with prominent dovetail joinery on the drawers and the carcass. Forged wrought iron drawer pulls are attached with integral spreader fingers bent tight against the inside of the drawer face.

Variations

You can always make the more traditional configuration for a low dresser with long drawers, or if you like the look, build the carcass with an opening top and front for stereo components.

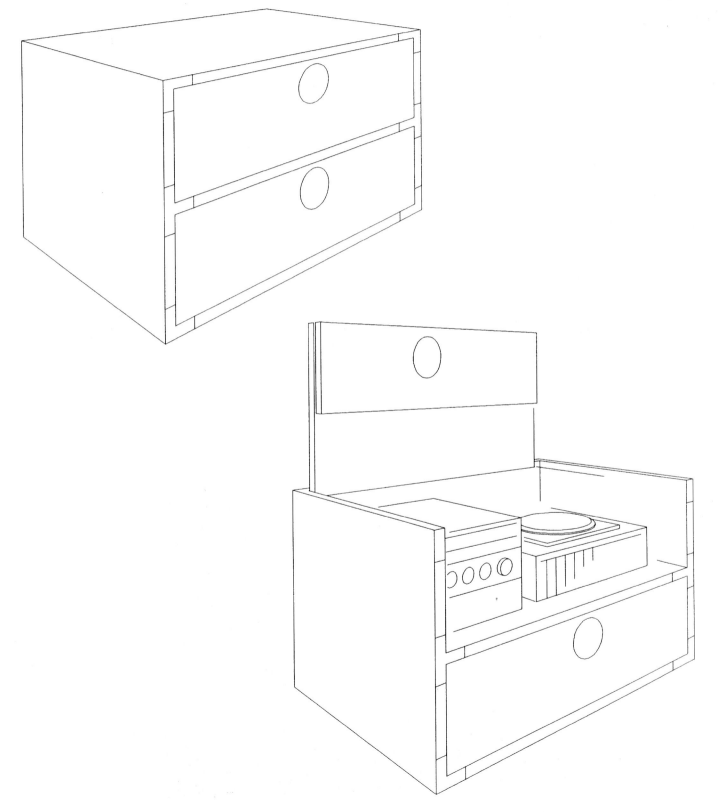

Gallery of Beautiful Wooden Chests

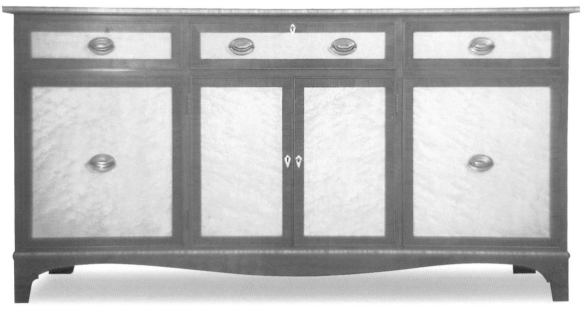

Eighteenth Century Federal Sideboard, page 124

Rustic Blanket Chest, page 35

Deacon's Bench, page 25

Cigar Humidor, page 99

Coin Collector's Chest, page 91

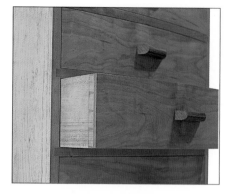

Lingerie Chest, page 83

Shaker Chest of Drawers, page 75

Williamsburg Gentleman's
Tools Chest, page 115

Craftsman Chairside Chest, page 51

Japanese Tansu, page 59

Spanish Cedar Chest, page 43

Jewelry Chest, page 107

The Builder's Thoughts

John exhibits his work at shows, not for award, but for exposure. Much of his custom work comes from orders through this activity. His pine entertainment center, displayed at the 1997 Design in Wood show in San Diego, prompted his invitation to be showcased in this book.

Meet the builder, E. John Gillis. Maybe he's wishing the Japanese designed in a more western style so he could use one of his fancy antique planes on the tansu.

Questions and Answers

Q Were the sample that the client showed in the photo and the piece that she wanted different?

A What she needed was an end table to go at the end of a couch. She wanted it to look like a tansu. It was my job to take her dimensions and make it look like a tansu.

Q You took the commission because you thought it would be interesting. Did it meet your expectations?

A It's just a completely different look than what I have done in the past. I am happy to add something different to my portfolio. It was a departure—not technique-wise but appearance wise.

Q Was the joinery a departure?

A Construction-wise it's just straightforward stuff. The tansu hardware was originally used to beef up the joinery. Now on mine, I beefed it up, making it more substantial in terms of my joinery. The hardware is decorative, as opposed to holding the piece together.

Q In this particular piece were there any major changes or challenges?

A No changes. It went together as planned. The challenge really is the depth of the piece—dovetails along a piece 32″ wide. There is a little bit of challenge in that process in terms of how do you hold the thing still. I didn't have a clamp or vise that would reach across 32″. And in my design process I was thinking expansion/contraction, so on the sides and top all the grain runs in the same direction. It's end-grain to end-grain dovetails.

Q Because you were dealing with a 32″-run, did you alter the size of your normal hand-cut dovetail?

A I spaced the dovetails proportionally and basically spaced them for aesthetics. I do all sizes. On drawers I cut little pins. I did them a little thicker here because that's more of a western thing, rather than tiny ones.

Q If you were to do another one right now, what would you do differently?

A When I dimension the stock for the drawers, I would dovetail it very quickly, instead of letting it sit for a day and a half and cup. But it all straightened out under weight and a change in humidity.

Q Any woodworkers out there that you have followed or admire?

A No. Isn't that a strange thing? I know Sam Maloof, but I've never wanted to do anything like his. I'm completely uneducated. I taught myself this stuff by the seat of my pants. I've read a lot, and go through a lot of trial and error. Maybe I like Greene and Greene, but as a style. And I have only done a half-dozen pieces in that style. Someone came to me one day and said "we want this" and it happened to be a Greene-and-Greene-style piece.

Q When you approach a piece to build, do you look at its function or its art form?

A The primary objective in design is to join functionality with aesthetics. If it's just aesthetics, it's only good to look at. If it's just functional, no one wants to look at it. So I actually view my design job as having to achieve both.

Q Do you consider material as a third element?

A Still just two elements. The material is just part of the aesthetics. I have read David Pye, *The Nature and Aesthetics of Design* and *The Nature and Aesthetics of Workmanship*. Fabulous books. He talks in deep detail about combining function and aesthetics. I guess I've been a little influenced by his writing. That's good reading for any woodworker who wants to do furniture.

Shaker Chest of Drawers

MIKE TRAUPEL • CHULA VISTA, CA

> *"I usually build Early American. This was my first Shaker. Shaker furniture is simple and functional—basic and rewarding."*
>
> MIKE TRAUPEL

Three Views

Woodchucks is Mike's woodworking business in Chula Vista, California. His products, and the reason for his invitation to participate in this book, were his cigar humidors. Like many woodworkers, he has since moved on to other things. Mike selected a Shaker chest of drawers project. This opened the opportunity for Ryan Cowell to show his stuff in humidors (project nine) and for Mike to build a needed piece of furniture for his home.

SPECIFICATIONS

Construction: Face frame with edge-glued case

Materials: Solid maple

Height: 52″

Width: 32⅝″

Depth: 20¼″

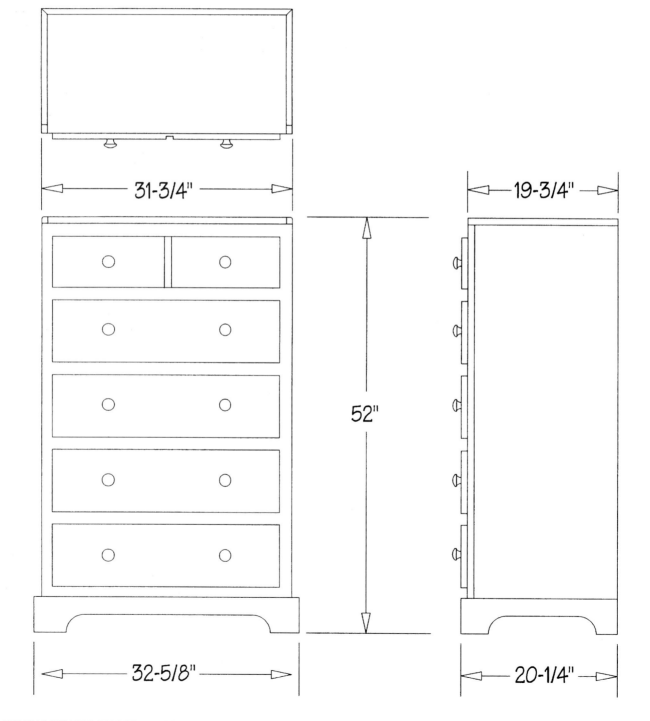

31-3/4″

19-3/4″

52″

32-5/8″

20-1/4″

Design Details

The drawer faces overlap the face frame. The top drawer is single, but dadoed to resemble a pair of drawers. The drawer sides, resawn from maple, are dovetailed to the drawer face.

These Incra-Jig-cut dovetails were made using a ½″ dovetail bit for the drawers. For those unfamiliar with the Incra System, precision alignment and micro adjustments make quick work of cutting dovetails.

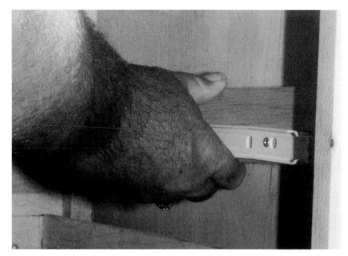

With the fixed side of the drawer slide screwed onto the spacer and the spacer front attached at the face, each drawer with the sliding rail installed is held hard against the face frame while the slide spacer is attached at the back.

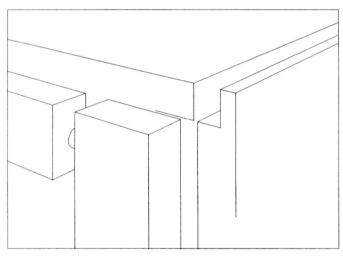

Sides routed with a ½″ rabbet form the corner joints. Corner cleats inside the carcass provide more gluing area. Fasteners through the cleats on the inside stiffen the shell.

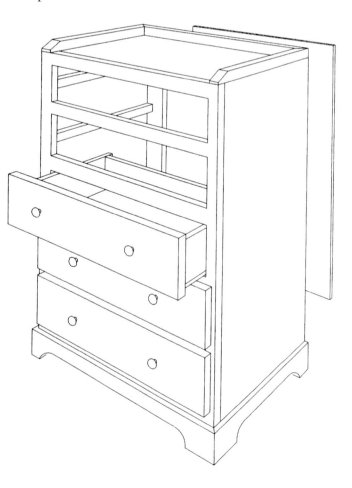

Work in Progress

The face frame was laid up with dowel-joined bearing rails spanning the width. The carcass was assembled and glued up flush with the face frame.

In preparation, individual planks were run through the thickness planer, trued on edge with a carbide-tip blade on the bench saw, marked matching grain, butt joined, then surface sanded.

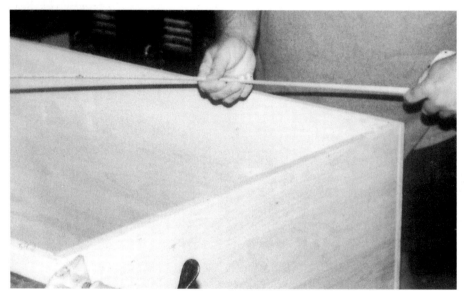

The parts were dry fit to match. When glue-up time comes, measuring the diagonals will ensure the carcass is square to the face frame.

The face frame is tacked into the carcass with a nail gun. Another method would be to add a cleat to the inside face for gluing and fastening the corner joint.

Scribe the apron design to the base. The base stands proud of the shell by the thickness of material, less the depth of a rabbet down about ½″ to receive the carcass. Corners are mitered, after some consideration of dovetails or box joints to add a bit of decorative detail. It's Shaker; who needs it?

Fit the mitered corner of the base. Mike marks his aprons to the inside to see first-hand where any supports might interfere or stand proud of the cut-out base.

Install the top molding rail. The three-sided cap rail (prior to rounding over) is checked and marked for length in position around the top. A little design is made on the fly.

Variation

Looking at the chest of drawers, which was approached more as cabinetry than furniture, the image of those great built-in walls of drawers in Shaker buildings comes to mind. The face frame approach would work here, but a separate top was added. The apron is shown cut into extended sides and at the front rather than nesting in a base frame. Either approach for the top or base works equally well. It's your preference for the look you want to achieve.

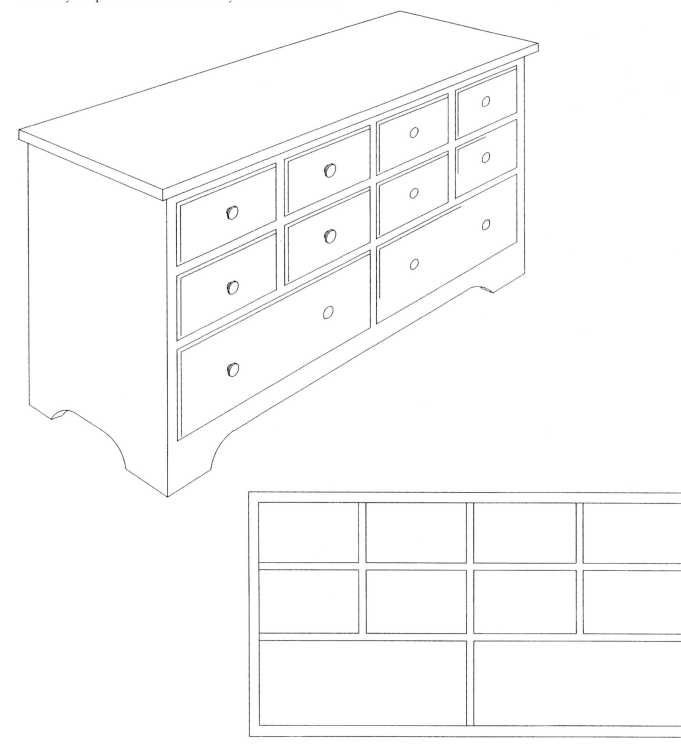

The Builder's Thoughts

Hitting the streets for the art fair market, Mike produces his signature humidors and more recently his oak ice box complete with authentic reefer hardware. His customers put this design to good use. It can be configured as a wine cellar, entertainment center, or just a storage cabinet.

Concentration is the look during the gluing-up of the face frame and carcass shell. Mike pays a local school for the use of space and tools not available in his home workshop. His time is equally shared between working at home and at the school.

Questions and Answers

Q Mike, you were asked to build this piece based on the work you do. What were your personal objectives for this piece?

A To try to keep the look as close to Shaker traditional as possible. And I wanted to build something out of solid maple.

Q What source did you use for inspiration?

A A couple photographs of Shaker furniture I found on the Internet. I saw what they had done, noted the parts I liked and created my own design from there. This was for me, so I made it functional for myself—the height and width fit the space and accommodates me.

Q From the initial design concept, were there any changes as you went along?

A The only change was adding some molding around the top. Originally I wasn't going to have anything there. And I worked out the apron shape I wanted around the base as I got into the project.

Q You used a production nail gun to attach the glued face frame. How else could you have fastened the assembly?

A If there were access, I would have fastened the frame from the back. Pneumatic finish nailers set a finish nail below the surface without damaging the surrounding area. The small hole is putty-filled and finished without much of a trace.

I also used the nail gun to fasten the carcass sides after glue-up, removed the clamps in sequence and set the joint with brads that hold the piece tight while the glue sets.

Q Is there anything you would do differently if you were to build this a second time?

A I might play around with mixing dovetail sizes in the drawers. Maybe intermix ¾″ with ⅜″ dovetails for a little more interest. Not hand cut, but using two dovetailing bits and two different settings on the Incra Jig.

And instead of mitering the bottom molding, I might use a box joint at the corners of the base—to make the base a bit more decorative. But that wouldn't follow the Shaker style.

Q What do you see as a variation to your design?

A Change the drawer fronts, or if someone wanted to deviate from the Shaker style, we could put legs on it, or go Victorian.

Q Are you influenced by any particular style, era or woodworker?

A I like it all. I like the Early American, Victorian and Shaker style. I like some of the Mission style—even Stickley furniture.

Q Are your designs primarily functional or an art form?

A I'd say 80% functional and 20% art.

Q If you had to put a name to your style, what would it be?

A Heinz (57 Varieties) . . . everything thrown in.

Q For this piece, did you do anything differently?

A I went with half-blind dovetails on the drawers instead of through dovetails because they were a little bit quicker.

Q What is your favorite tool, either here or at the school—the one you use most?

A I spend a lot of time with the router. I do most of my dadoing and rabbeting with it. I've got four routers, and three of them are Porter Cable. I use the Incra Jig and templates to cut the dovetails.

Q What's the next tool you would buy?

A I should replace a little DeWalt planer, but I'd really like to get a panel saw. I don't do that much plywood but they're handy to have. You also can attach a router to it.

Lingerie Chest

STAN PIECHOTA • HUNTINGTON BEACH, CA

"I used the same radius on everything. The top stands proud by ¼" from the sides and the curved face, which carries through on drawer fronts, bearer frames and facing edges of the two sides."

STAN PIECHOTA

Three Views

Based on his work seen in two cherry curio cabinets exhibited at the 1997 Design in Wood show in San Diego, Stan was invited to build something for this book. Early, with the want-list wide open, he selected a Shaker dresser. Later on a chiffonier was mentioned. So he did a little research and remarked that he could get excited about a lingerie chest. Results show he got both excited and inspired.

Stan veneered cherry on cherry for continuous figuring over the seven bow-front drawer faces. A vacuum press was put to good use to draw and glue veneer against the curved drawer faces.

The chest back is ⅝″ plywood veneered in cherry. A tongue lets into a matching dado up the sides. The back is slipped into place from the bottom fitting into two lateral braces at the top and fastened by the bottom brace.

The drawer sides are cut to the depth of the chest, which serve as the stop for the flush drawer faces.

The bearing rails/frames are let into the chest sides with a sliding dovetail, and their faces are cut to the curvature of the drawers. The top is fastened through and to the top bearer. The backside of the rosewood drawer pulls are pattern milled for a flush fit to the radius.

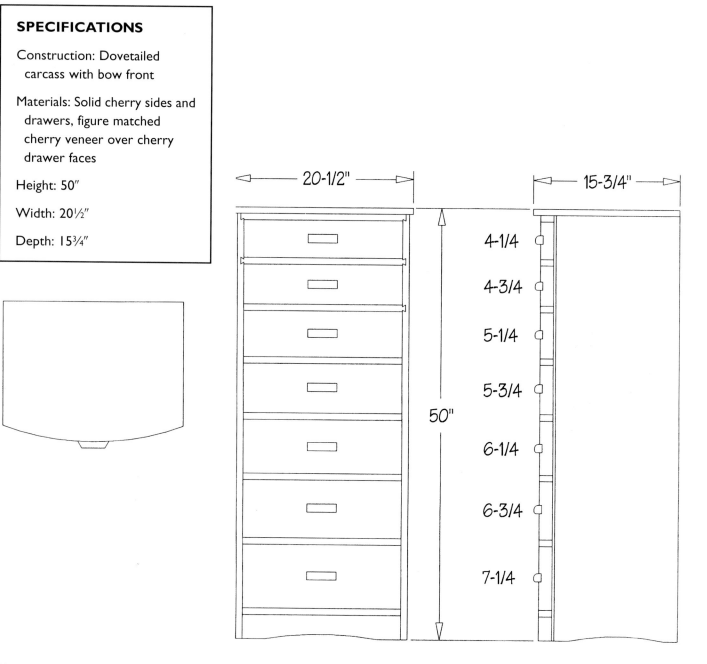

SPECIFICATIONS

Construction: Dovetailed carcass with bow front

Materials: Solid cherry sides and drawers, figure matched cherry veneer over cherry drawer faces

Height: 50″

Width: 20½″

Depth: 15¾″

Design Details

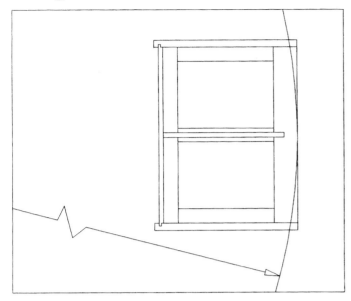

Bearing frames for the seven drawers are all comprised of front and back rails (width) dadoed with a slot for the tongue cut into three front-to-back members. The third (center) brace is captured but not glued within the frame. It is finally glued in place after the drawer is fitted and the drawer guide position is known.

A router jig was made for cutting a curve inside and outside the drawer fronts. Stan decided to leave the backside square to the drawer which accentuates the curvature at the face. It gives the drawers a positive, substantial feel.

Drawer sides and back are of cherry, resawn to ½″; bottoms are ¼″ cherry plywood. Stan is of the school that different woods used in the face and drawer sides result in different rates of expansion and contraction which could weaken or split the weaker member.

Unsure of base treatment at the outset, Stan opted to cut the same radius he used on the bow front face to cut an arc in the straight sides and into the bow front apron, forming integral bracket "feet" at the corners.

Detail of the Lingerie Chest

Work in Progress

With a little preparation and planning, a jig was made to step and guide the router across the chest sides to cut the sliding dovetail grooves for the drawer bearer frames.

Shaping dovetails in assembled drawer bearer frames is a simple cut on the router table. The frames are a manageable size, otherwise the dovetail would be cut before the frame is assembled.

The bow faces on drawers were first rough-cut on the bandsaw, then, using an arced router jig, the drawer faces were milled and dressed to the radius. Parallel tracks flanking the drawer heights are spanned by an extended router base that rides on top of the arcs. Note the radius is cut for the inside (backside) bow, but Stan later opted to leave the inside straight.

Cut dovetails into the drawer side. The dovetail pattern changes slightly with the progressive drawer height. Filling the space between the top and bottom dovetail are two, three or four dovetails evenly spaced within drawer height.

After marking off the run length, a coving bit shapes the backside finger pull. Before these are bevel-cut into lengths, the straight outer face is bullnosed into a half-round pull.

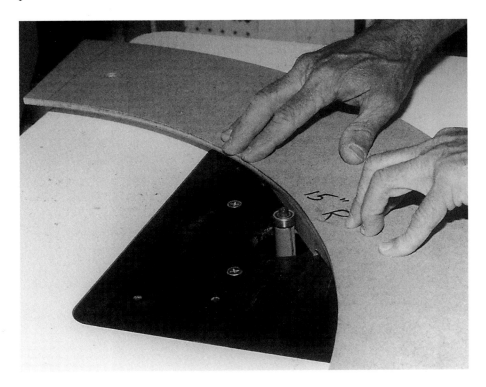

Use a patterning bit to transfer radius to drawer pulls. With the pulls cut to length, the backside is shaped to the radius using a 60″ radius template (instead of the 15″ shown in this illustration). The drawer pull ends were then beveled, finished, sanded and attached.

Variations

Keeping with Stan's look, a minor variation on the progression of drawer heights is an option. His drawer height progression is in ½″ increments and entirely pleasing to the eye. The Hambridge Progression, shown here, is just another method you might consider for designing progressive drawer heights.

A lingerie chest should be delicate unless you plan to use it for your skivvies or boxer shorts, in which case it would be a skivvy chest (except in England, where it would store anything in the maid's chambers).

A major variation would be to make the seven drawers equal in height, and build a semainier—a French chest of seven drawers of equal size for a daily change of bed linens.

Bearing frames could be used here. They could be either let into a dado or a sliding dovetail. The bearers, runners and guides could be installed as piece parts as well. Full-lap drawer faces could span the width covering the sides and bearers, and drawer pulls might be integral, cut-out in the drawer face, either at the top or bottom, opposite the edge that laps each bearer.

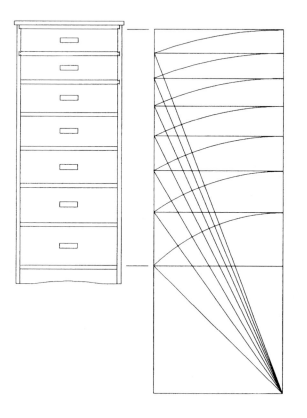

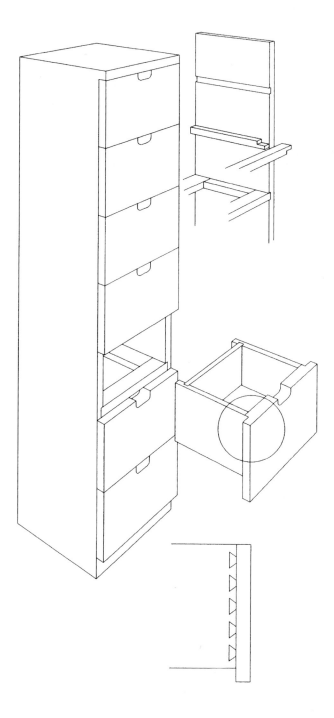

The Builder's Thoughts

Stan was a hobbyist during his 40-year career as Engineering and Construction Manager for Texaco. Between career tasks, Stan pursued his woodworking hobby handed down from his father, also an accomplished woodworker. After retirement three years ago, Stan became more serious about woodworking and set out to expand and equip his shop.

Stan Piechota pushed the idea for a lingerie chest to expand his skills and to create something interesting to work on. The bow-front drawers he came up with not only put a new spin on an old form, they add a new degree of craftsmanship.

Questions and Answers

Q What were your objectives for the piece and for yourself?
A I wanted something I could put in the next Design in Wood show, and to experiment with the curved-drawer front design. For myself? I hope to sell it.

Q How did you arrive at the initial design concept?
A I did a little looking at retail furniture catalogs to see what proportions they used on lingerie chests. None I saw had the curved front. I just wanted to apply that concept to this piece.

Q How did you approach the bow-front design?
A I used the same radius on everything. The top stands proud by ¼″ from the sides and the curved face, which carries through on drawer fronts, bearer frames and facing edges of the two sides.

Q Where did you pick up the process of making the divider frames instead of adding bearers and guides piece by piece?
A I guess I had seen furniture with the sliding dovetail in the front. I have normally built a bureau that way, but I hadn't used the sliding dovetail.

Q Any major challenges in construction, materials, finish?

A No. I think everything went pretty much the way I planned it, other than taking a lot more time. That always happens.

Q What would you do differently in a second item?

A I cut the relief in the drawer bottom, whereas I should have cut it in the bearing rail, so that the wear point is raised from the face rather than on the facing edge.

Q How would you describe your design style?

A Mission-contemporary versus traditional.

Q Are you influenced by a particular furniture style, era or woodworker?

A Probably Mission-type furniture. I like the cabinets that Krenov makes. My interest lies in cabinet-type furniture. I do more contemporary—very little or nothing in the more traditional furniture styles.

Q Do you approach your design with function first or more as an art form?

A Probably 50/50. You have to make it functional. In the curio cabinets for the design show, I made the openings such that they would display the contents—putting enough glassed area in the doors so you could really see inside.

Q Other than the curved face, did you use any different methods, joiner work, materials, finishes that you had not tried before?

A The sliding dovetails on the drawer dividers worked out. I would use that again. It kept the case pretty square, and I could fit all the drawer fronts without the back on. Actually when I put the back on, a couple of the drawers got a little bit of a tweak, so I had to do some more fitting on the drawer fronts. If I had to do it again, I'd make sure that the back was square, somehow, without the piece in there. It's pretty difficult to fit the drawers with the back on.

Q You mentioned earlier that you do very little hand work. How about the dovetails in the drawers?

A They were partially hand-cut. I don't know if you would consider those, or the drawer pulls, hand work. It was more machine work.

Q When we first talked, you were deciding whether to add a wider base. Why did you opt for the bottom treatment shown?

A I guess just for simplicity—to go along with the top. I used the same radius, but I probably should have exaggerated the arc a bit more. On carpeting, the detail is lost. It's more pronounced when placed on a hard floor. It doesn't sink into the carpet pile.

Q Did you bevel sides straight or continue the arc?

A I just cut at about a 7° bevel to match the bowed front.

Q Was the finish used on this chest the same you used on the curio cabinet?

A It was finished with a mixture of ⅓ linseed oil, ⅓ tung oil and ⅓ turpentine. The final coating was beeswax/linseed oil. I bought that at Restoration Hardware—Natural Creamy Beeswax. I rubbed that in with #0000 steel wool.

Q We talked about the progression of drawer height. How did you come up with the ½″ progression?

A I wanted to make it 50″ high, starting with the top drawer of minimal but functional depth, then I worked in the number of drawers to something aesthetically pleasing. And I knew I wanted about a 3″ apron.

Q You have a well-equipped shop. What is your next tool buy?

A I would probably upgrade the table saw, and maybe buy a 15½″ heavy-duty surface planer to upgrade the smaller one.

Q What is your favorite tool out there? What do you reach for first or most?

A I guess the table saw, and then the router table. With those two things, you can do almost anything.

Q Any woodworking tips or message for the reader?

A One thing I've learned doing woodworking is to progress through a project, taking dimensions as you go, instead of cutting a whole batch of wood to what you think are the right dimensions. I never make drawers until I'm done with the case—that kind of thing.

Coin Collector's Chest

GARY MCNEIL • SAN DIEGO, CA

> "The design was a collaboration of thoughts. The pyramid shape was the client's concept, and then I came up with the idea to do the stepped roman ogee sides to form the pyramid. It seems to work out pretty classically for the shape."
>
> GARY MCNEIL

Two Views

The project shown is a coin collector's chest that not only stores but displays rare coin collections of serious numismatists. Mahogany (Honduras) is the species of choice for these cases since that wood has both hardness and beauty and, most importantly, lower (and hopefully non-existent) outgassing properties than other more oily woods. The outgassing can prove harmful to a coin's natural patina.

This design comes with a hinged lid, lift-out tray with a drawer below, and has an ornate marquetry panel. The panel incorporates some bas relief and solid gold ornamentation—two angels and a griffin standing guard over its contents. A unique drawer-locking mechanism is included in case the golden figures fail to perform their duties. Gary was asked to contribute to this book based on his marquetry which is put to good use in his design.

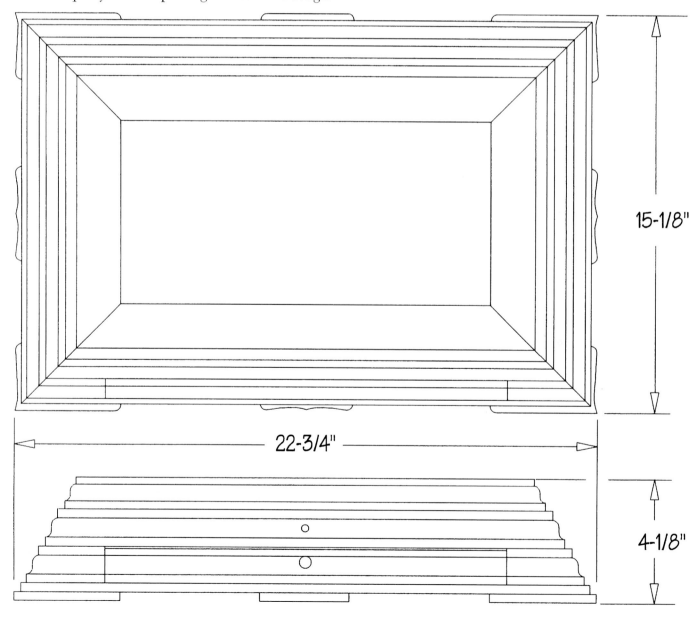

15-1/8"

22-3/4"

4-1/8"

Design Details

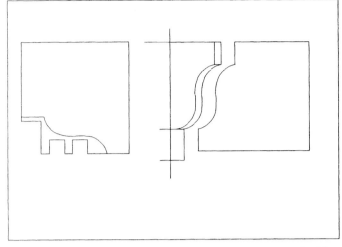

First kerfing into the ogee profile with a dado blade and table saw makes quick work for the roman ogee router bit used in sticking the edges of the tiers.

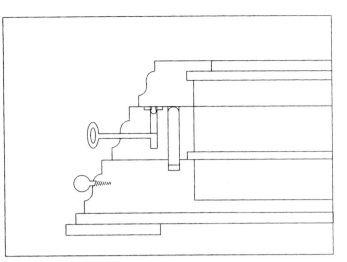

The lock mechanism is a jewelry-box-type key lock for the lid. When closed and locked, the lid presses a spring-loaded plunger into a mating bushing, thereby locking the drawer. This is released when the top is opened.

A pair of gold-plated French quadrant hinges holds the top hard to the shell and opens to a designed stop of 90°. Note the holes for the spring-loaded plunger.

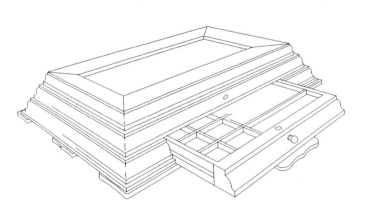

Collector's Coin Chest

Work in Progress

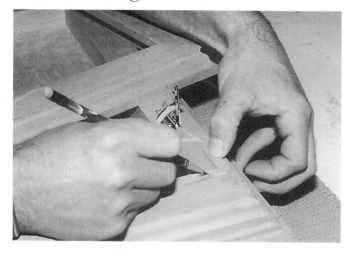

The template for the French quadrant hinge position is traced onto the frame and lid. Three shallow holes aligned within the scribe marks are chiseled to let in the right-angle flange. Using a Dremel tool, a length is bored to a 1″-depth for the travel of the retractable arm.

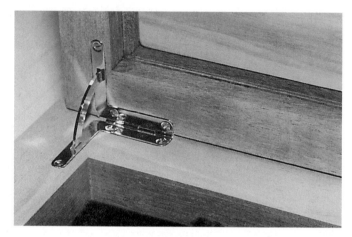

The quad hinge is mortised into the frame and lid. The commercial templates available for hinge installation would need to be modified—indexed to this unique configuration.

The compartmentalized tray is fully lined in velvet. The tray begins with strips of plywood the width of the compartments with frets let into dadoes along the run. They are spaced to form the square. These are separated by longitudinal divider strips to close each compartment.

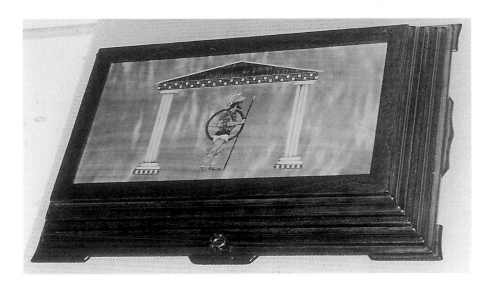

The evolution of this design began with a single tier, opening to a lift-out tray above a compartmented case.

The middle version shown here has the one drawer below and a prototype is in the works for a larger two-drawer. When asked if it will grow more, Gary began his answer with "I hope not."

Applying the onlay over his marquetry includes the gable above the pediment, the plinth (or base for the griffin and columns) and the staircase. These stand proud to complement and protect the golden figures.

Variation

There are some classic Japanese tansu coffers suitable for keeping valuables or used to store those not-so-valuables. This example is a more traditional shape, and with the tansu hardware mentioned in project five, a woodworker could put together some interesting designs for small table-top chests. If ambitious, you could reproduce the larger Asian design of a wheeled chest if you need to "coffer" a large stash.

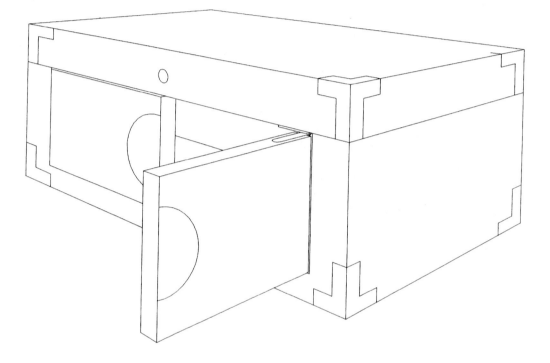

The Builder's Thoughts

Gary has been plying his marquetry for close to 25 years, working independently on decorative projects and in collaboration with colleagues. One of his recent works, paired with Tony Fisher in the 1997 Design in Wood show, prompted his invitation to contribute to this book.

Gary McNeil worked collaboratively with a client to meld a basic pyramid design with other classic architectural details that fit perfectly with the chest's function of storing and displaying rare coins.

Questions and Answers

Q When did you start marquetry and woodworking?
A It was right around the same time. My first endeavors in woodworking were as a laborer at a construction site—not a whole lot of woodworking but a lot of laboring. I went into framing from there and did that for a number of years to make a living while I did marquetry on the side. I got into finish work, cabinet work, and continued to do marquetry on the side and put the effort into making marquetry more of a livelihood than the other. It's gradually getting there.

Q You're collaborating with other furniture makers as well?
A I do that on a number of occasions. That's pretty fun and interesting, and I've got my own shop set up at home which gives me more opportunity to take in more work.

Q We mentioned that Honduras mahogany is the wood of choice.
A As far as I know—that's the word I got from the fellow I'm doing these for. We did the first prototype in cherry and found out that Honduras mahogany is what collectors prefer for coin keeping. It doesn't affect the patina on the ancient coins being stored, so that's what we're using now.

Q You're working with a client on this coin chest. Was this his initial design or your initial design?
A The design was a collaboration of thoughts. The pyramid shape was the client's concept, and then I came up with the idea to do the stepped roman ogee sides to form the pyramid. It seems to work out pretty classically for the shape.

Q Any alteration during construction?
A The scope tended to evolve and enlarge. When we first started, it was just basically one layer. You open the lid and there was one lift-out coin tray over a compartmented bottom, and that was it. It was my client's idea to expand on that and add capacity for more coins. With that in mind, we went with the additional drawer for more coin capacity and display. The two models I'm doing now have one with a single drawer under the original concept, and one with two drawers.

Q What, if any, challenges occurred in the construction in this design?
A Beyond the challenge of putting together something unique and functional—it has to be functional at the same time—there was the challenge of production. We're going to have a series of six prototypes, and he is going to market them to collectors of ancient coins. So, hopefully, we'll be making and selling a whole bunch more. It was, and is, an interesting challenge to make copious notes so I can repeat my set-ups as much as possible and cut down on the production time involved.

Q What is your favorite tool?
A In my style of marquetry—cutting—it would have to be my knife. The other school of marquetry cutting is the saw-cutting technique that a lot of people use. But I learned with a knife; it works for me, and that's what I've stuck with.

I bought a knife handle from a fellow in England, another marqueteer, Ernie Ives. He has a specialty handle designed for a comfortable grip. I use a No. 11 scalpel blade, like the X-acto No. 11 blade, which I used for a long time. Then I discovered and changed to the scalpel blade because it's a little better steel and it keeps an edge longer.

Cigar Humidor

RYAN COWELL • POWAY, CA

> *"I wanted to do a bowed front mainly because I wanted to get out of rectilinear work for a while and do something different—to put some curves in my work. But without a vacuum press, it would have been a little more work than I'm ready for."*
>
> RYAN COWELL

Three Views

I'll take full responsibility for the larger than normal scale of this humidor. While prospecting for chest builders, I found a smaller version of Ryan's humidor handiwork on display at the Woodworkers' Store in San Diego—his place of employment. "Something like this one?" he asked.

Wanting to keep some distinction between boxes and chests, I asked if he would make a more chest-like humidor for this book, and he agreed. Now I feel obligated to find a very heavy smoker or a purveyor of cigars to buy this piece.

Certain woods work well in their niche application: Aromatic cedar in the blanket chests protect moth-prone apparel; Honduras mahogany in the coin case is inert—no outgassing to ruin the rare coin's patina. Spanish cedar is great for humidors. It doesn't mildew (much) in the humid enclosure, and its own mild aroma mixes with and mellows the aging cigars.

SPECIFICATIONS

Construction: Veneered casework

Materials: Spanish cedar veneered with macassar ebony and bird's-eye maple

Height: 9″

Width: 24″

Depth: 11¾″

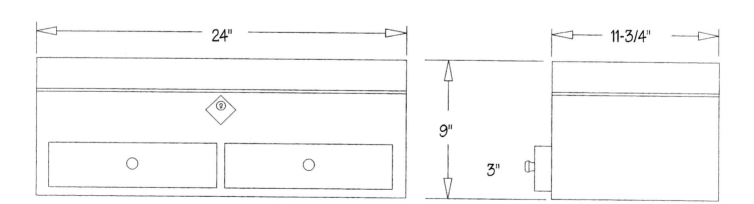

Design Details

Circulation is important inside a humidor, especially a chest of more generous proportion. Note the hole pattern, movable dog-bone separators, and the hygrometer to tell you how well it is working.

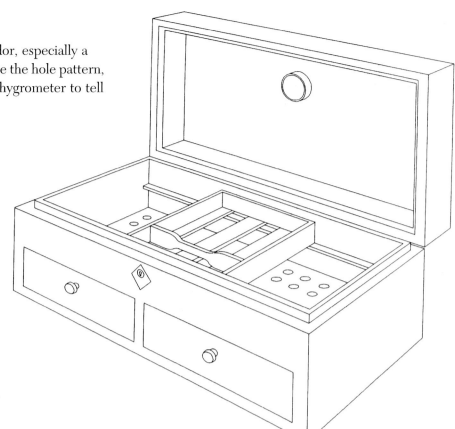

Quadrant hinges provide a positive action to the boxed lid and allow clearance for a coved seal extending uninterrupted across the back.

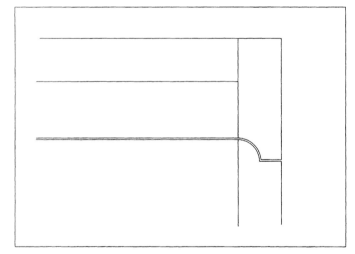

Good seals are important in a humidor—to keep it humid inside. The lid has a concave rabbet milled around the inside edges that matches the convex bead routed into the case. When a drawer (next illustration) is removed, the lid closes with a thud. With the drawers closed, the thud became a whoosh (in highly technical terms).

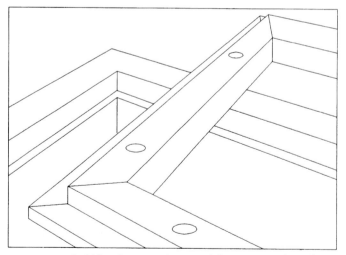

Drawers are held hard against the top of the casing, riding along overhead runners and into a facing lip that provides a seal across the drawer front. The drawer height and width nearly fill the face frame, with as little clearance as necessary for opening. This design eliminates the need for a center divider between the drawer casings for drawer runners, which aids circulation.

Work in Progress

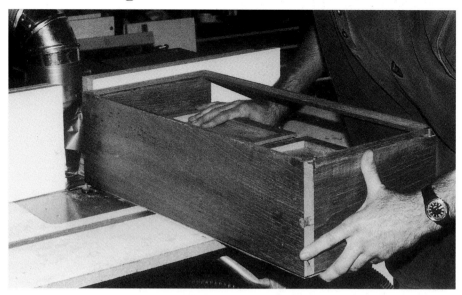

A shaper-cut rabbet and bead seals the lid to the case. The convex side of the seal is routed into the assembled casing. "I actually milled the lip to create the seal, instead of doing what most people are doing and putting an insert inside. Milled from solid ¾" cedar. It was kind of a challenge to get the lid to fit tightly."

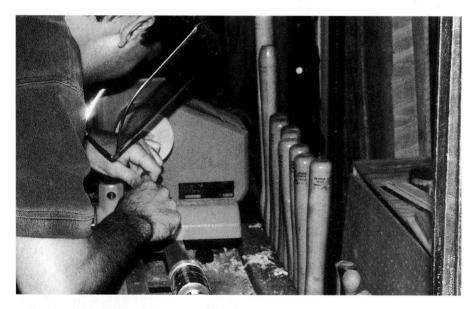

The recess for the metal keyhole escutcheon was bored (lathe-turned) in the inlay piece, chucked into the lathe faceplate and turned to a diameter not matching any drill bit in sight.

Dado the drawer sides accurately. "... Every time I build something I learn something, like when you're making drawers, cutting all the sides at the same time to make sure they're all milled to the same degree so you don't have to reset everything."

Check the hanging drawer runner fit. The seals shown in the design detail must be a fairly close fit to keep humid air inside, but still allow some flow. The hanging drawer with the forward seal fits tightly into the drawer face.

Book-match the veneer for the top. Macassar ebony veneer is highly figured in stripes of browns and blacks. Either a book-match or, at a minimum, a natural coloration on either side of the joint is important. Once found, the flitches are joined together by tape, ready for final gluing.

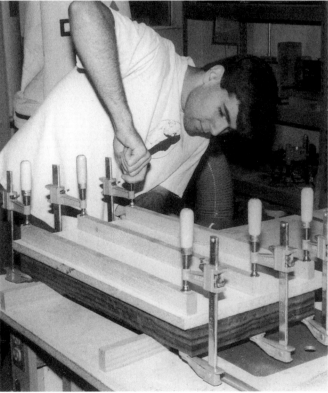

Apply even clamp pressure on glued-up veneer. To apply even pressure across the length being clamped, use slightly bowed blocks clamped at both ends.

Variations

The first is more of a case-like chest with lift lid and two drawers. This is suitable for most smokers.

Ryan's design changed from a bow front, to the straight front he built. I will get lazy and present Ryan's original design as another variation. Designing for concept only, we don't need that vacuum press.

The drawers can still seal, as he devised on the sample project. However, one might combine some techniques from the Lingerie Chest (project seven) bow front facing in this variation or build a smaller jig to cut and surface a bowed face for this humidor using the router as shown in that same project.

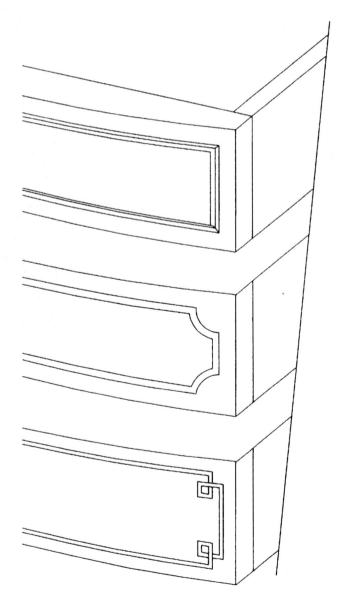

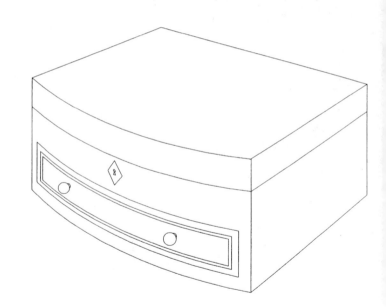

The Builder's Thoughts

With four years' experience, Ryan is a relative newcomer to woodworking. Young and ambitious, he began plying his interest in woodworking by building housings for car stereos. "Mainly sub-woofer boxes. Pretty simple boxes to begin with."

As a relatively new woodworker, Ryan Cowell is well aware of the concept of starting out simple. As most casework furniture is really just large boxes, mastering small boxes and moving to chests, like his humidor, was a good progression toward larger pieces for Ryan.

Questions and Answers

Q What was your next project after the sub-woofers?
A I wanted an entertainment center, but I didn't like any you could find in the store, so I designed my own, for basically everything you need in an entertainment center—TV, VCR, CD player, tapes.

Q What about training?
A I had a little woodworking training in school—only in middle school—seventh and eighth grade. I did little projects at that age. I did attend the woodworking program at Palomar College, but found the line was too long waiting for the table saw, so I convinced my parents that one of the three bays of their garage should be a workshop.

Q Other than my twisting your arm to build a larger version of your cigar humidor, what were your reasons or objectives for building the piece?
A I wanted to get some more experience veneering. The way I look at it, every time I build something I learn something, like when you're making drawers, cutting all the sides at the same time to make sure they're all milled to the same degree so you don't have to reset everything, and like when you're using veneering techniques, and this humidor has a lot of veneer work.

Q This is similar to the smaller humidor you have on display in the store?
A The two drawers on the bottom are different. That is the main difference.

Q Do you intend to sell this piece when we're finished with it?
A I hope to.

Q Your initial design concept was the bowed front. Was that following any particular design that you had seen?
A I wanted to do a bowed front mainly because I wanted to get out of rectilinear work for a while and do something different—to put some curves in my work. But it turned out that without a vacuum press, it was a little more work than I'm ready for.

Q So the concept was altered during construction because? . . .
A I wasn't equipped. But I was set up to veneer flat surfaces.

Q You mentioned the presses you are using on the flat work are slightly bowed. Where did you see that technique?

A I don't remember exactly where, but one of the books or magazines showed how to apply even pressure along the length of a clamping block by using slightly bowed clamping blocks.

Q Any major challenges in construction, materials, finish?

A Not really as far as the piece itself. But it is a major challenge setting up an efficient shop.

Q So what I see here today is a work in progress?

A You have only so much room to squeeze in as many tools as you can, then you have to store things like clamps, lumber, work and storage space and still leave room for my parents' cars.

Q What would you do differently in a second item?

A I'd probably work with a customer on the design. I don't think many people are going to need a humidor this large. Maybe I'd make it just half the width, with one drawer underneath, and probably use a different veneer as a variation on the design.

Q Was the style a departure, and if so, why?

A I don't really have a style. In most of my work I just do what I want to do, or what I think looks good based on the piece and its function. When I can, I try to use exotic woods, to do things a little bit differently than products you could find in a store.

Q Was the other piece you have in the book, the Jewelry Chest (project ten), designed differently than the humidor?

A That was entirely different. As part of building a shop, you get new tools and with new tools you can do different things. I got a band saw so I could cut curves, so I was able to curve some legs, kind of an oriental look to the Jewelry Chest. It was a change in my style, but it was something I liked. I liked the way it looked, and I think it worked pretty well.

Q Are your designs primarily functional or primarily an art form?

A That depends on what the item is. If it's an entertainment center, you have to go towards the function. To oversimplify, all it does is hold a TV. If you just want to make a box to put a TV in, that is the least you can do, or you can add some nice moldings, frame and panel construction; there are various things you can do. When designing, I take everything into account; its function, and what I could possibly add on to decorate it.

Q Do you step back and say "I like the way that works," with the equal pleasure of saying "I like the way the whole thing looks?"

A The jewelry box was one of the first things about which I could say "I like the way it looks and works." I like the way it looks, and it is functional; it serves its purpose.

Q Any different methods used in joiner work, materials, finishes?

A With the humidor I actually milled the lip from solid ¾″ cedar to create the seal, instead of doing what most people are doing and putting an insert inside. It was kind of a challenge to get the lid to fit tightly.

Q Will you go into marquetry?

A I don't have the patience for that at this point.

Q What is your next tool buy?

A A vacuum press would make veneering on curved forms a lot easier; that's something I would like to get into, but I probably won't get that until I get a bigger shop. I don't have the space for it. The other thing I would like to make is a thickness sander so I can slice my own veneer, now that I've got the riser on the band saw.

Q What is your favorite tool? What do you use most?

A I think just the basic chisel. You can do a lot with it . . . cut mortises, inset hinges, trim things flush. You get to hold it in your hand and it doesn't have a power cord.

Q Are there any woodworking tips or message for the reader?

A One thing I would probably tell a beginning woodworker is to have fun with it. That's what I think it's best for. If you're starting a business, I think that might detract from some of the fun you have with it. And try something new. I got into veneering just two projects before this one, and since then I have been veneering a lot of them. It was something new, something you can add, and I don't like to stay with the same look for too long. It's not that I'll be veneering forever, but I will be incorporating it into my work.

Jewelry Chest

RYAN COWELL • POWAY, CA

> *"The jewelry box was one of the first things I could say I liked the way it looked and worked. It is functional, it serves its purpose, and at the same time it is beautiful."*
>
> RYAN COWELL

Three Views

As Ryan was building the humidor (project nine), he reflected on a recent project, a jewelry chest commissioned by a neighbor for a Christmas gift. Instead of reconstructing that process for the book, Ryan elected to take some time off from the Woodworkers' Store to build another jewelry chest to enter in the Design in Wood show. Both deadlines coincided—the manuscript to the publisher and photos for the entry form, so we got our in-progress shots and he made the entry deadline.

This piece is similar, but as with most projects, the chance to do a follow-up piece results in refinement. Here is his fine, refined piece.

SPECIFICATIONS

Construction: Veneered casework

Materials: Bird's-eye maple, veneered Finnish birch plywood sides and solid top, cocobolo legs, apron, drawer guides and peg rack, Brusso hardware

Height: 11¼"

Width: 15"

Depth: 10"

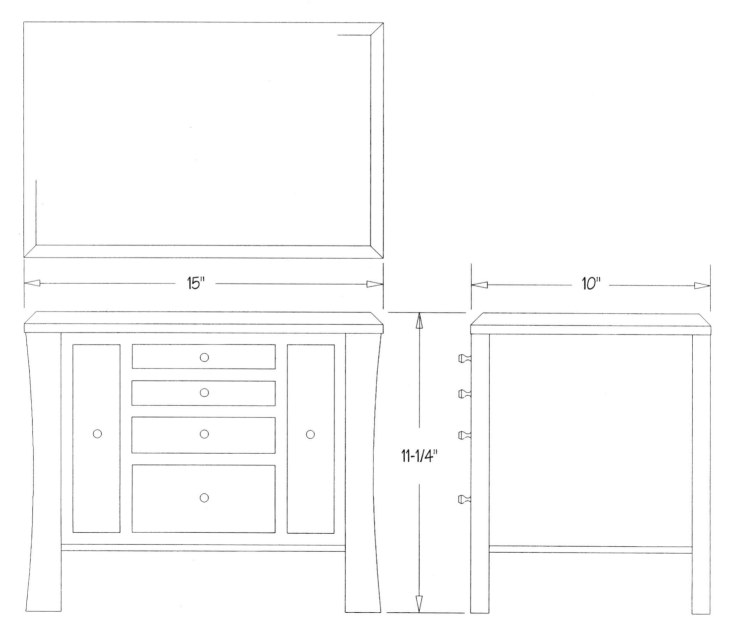

Design Details

Sliding dovetail rail guides in cocobolo add design detail to the vertical hanging chain drawer. Cocobolo accent is also used for the chain rack (with brass pegs) and the bottom rail to confine and capture escaping jewelry.

A tray in the lower drawer slides along side rails or can be easily removed to search for a missing earring.

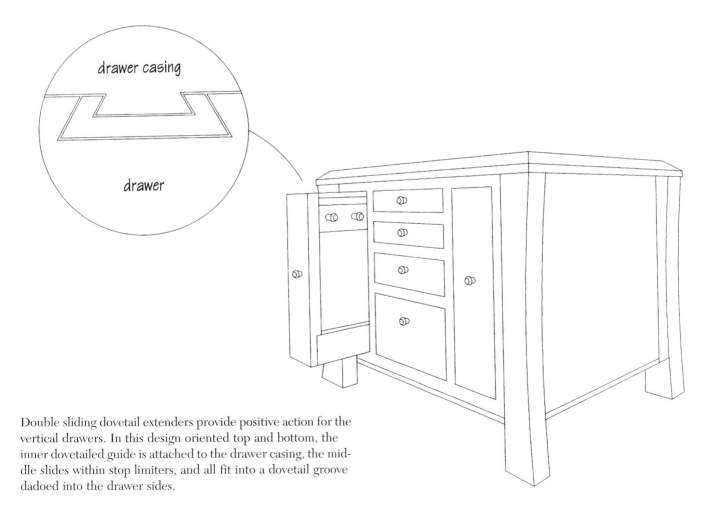

Double sliding dovetail extenders provide positive action for the vertical drawers. In this design oriented top and bottom, the inner dovetailed guide is attached to the drawer casing, the middle slides within stop limiters, and all fit into a dovetail groove dadoed into the drawer sides.

Work in Progress

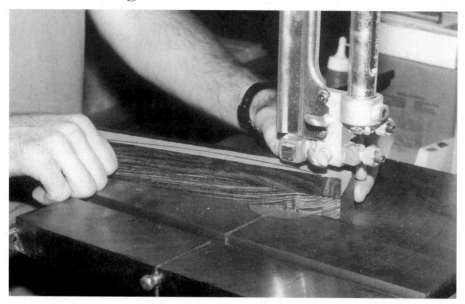

With the addition of a band saw, complete now with extenders for cutting veneers, Ryan is into more curved forms in his work. The simple curve of the oriental-style cocobolo leg is key in this design.

Prior to rounding over the edges, the surfaces are sanded with a spindle sander to remove the tool marks and true the arc of the flanking legs.

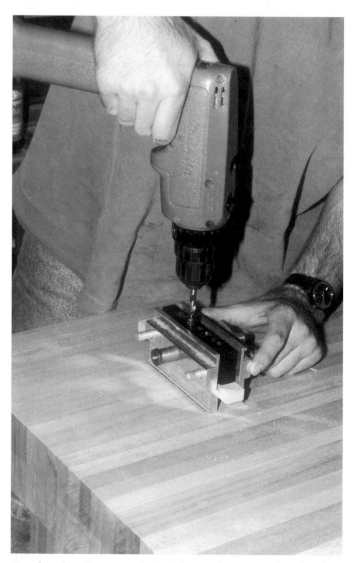

Use doweling jig to match-drill drawer-bearing rails and stiles in the face frame.

Before assembling the carcass, check for fit of the carcass sides and face frame prior to veneering and gluing up.

Mill dovetail sides in drawer guide. Vertical drawers for hanging chains and necklaces run along two-piece extenders at the top and bottom. Milling the cocobolo to slide in the dovetail in the drawers and the fixed piece in the drawer casing calls for close tolerances for a close slip fit of all parts.

Test fitting drawer runner extension in the drawer casing indicates where to locate the stops for the sliding rail member.

Variation

Since I couldn't talk any woodworker into making a jewelry armoire, I guess one proposed as a variation might start you thinking about making this popular form of a jewelry chest.

Somewhere between full size and miniature, this small case is perfect for reproducing favorite furniture styles from the past or to express your creative ideas on something less demanding than furniture. Maybe a Biedermeier, an Empire, Craftsman, or even another tansu are all good candidates for a jewelry armoire.

The variation shown is based on a fairly rectilinear carcass flanked with highly figured burl or spalted wood. This might be perhaps 15″ to 20″ tall.

The inside case is square-cut joinery flanked by some "killer" burl, solid wood or plywood sides. A natural edge would be nice if it is practical for you. A burl edge could be shaped and ebonized in contrast with the rectilinear face frame and inner carcass.

The Builder's Thoughts

Ryan, at 22, has a direction and a drive in woodworking. His accumulation of tools and a new laminated maple workbench that he built between projects is indicative of his dedication to the craft.

After building the Cigar Humidor featured in the last project, Ryan Cowell built the Jewelry Chest for the Design in Wood show. This chest represents the evolution of woodworkers and their projects, as Ryan refined the design of a recent project for the show and this book.

Questions and Answers

Q What differences are there between the Humidor and the Jewelry Chest?

A I am using plywood in the Jewelry Chest, so I don't have to worry about wood movement like I did in the Humidor. The design itself appears a little bit more oriental. I seem to be developing a growing interest in oriental furniture and design.

Q Are you influenced by a particular style, era or woodworker?

A I think one of the reasons I went more toward the oriental look was some research I did on Greene and Greene. A lot of their work inspired me. That might have been how I came up with that jewelry chest.

Q So do you like the Craftsman style itself or the simplicity of Greene and Greene?

A One of the things they did was pay attention to detail, and that is one of the things I try to do. Since I'm not doing this for profit, right now doing things for myself or for family, I can take my time on it, and I try to pay attention to the detail.

Q How have you used materials in the Jewelry Chest?

A The Finnish birch plywood sides, the back and drawer bottoms, and everything will be covered with veneer or black velvet lining. Actually the interior divider which houses the drawer runners is plywood as well. The sides and back will be veneered and the drawer bottoms will have velvet over them. I will use bird's-eye maple veneer, which is a nice contrast with the cocobolo legs.

Q And the top?

A The top is solid bird's-eye maple with a wide chamfer around.

Q How is the top attached?

A I used desk-top tabbing fasteners let into the top edge of the sides. The theory is the dual tabs hinged on a pivot bushing allow lateral movement of expanding wood as the tab swings on its axis with the seasonal changes but will hold the top tight vertically.

Q What about the hardware?

A Not much is needed of the conventional type. I'm using Brusso knobs for the drawers and the row of pegs in the chain drawers.

Q What were your objectives for this piece?

A I was commissioned to build a similar one, a prototype, and I really liked the way it turned out. So I did another to enter in this year's Design in Wood show.

Q Is this the first time you've used the sliding dovetail as a drawer runner?

A Yes, and it has gone pretty well, considering I am using just a shop-made fence. An after-market fence would probably make the process easier as far as fine adjustments, but I didn't run into any problem that's worth spending $300.

Q Style was pretty well covered in the earlier piece, what can we say?

A Styles are changing. For the past couple of months I've been reading a lot about Japanese joinery, Japanese tools. Their use of tools has really sparked an interest. On one of the things I recently built, the chisels I was using wouldn't have held an edge—the Japanese chisels did. I guess that style is where my future designs will be headed.

Williamsburg Gentleman's Tool Chest

ANDREW McPHERSON • DEL MAR, CA

> "It seems that most people on the West Coast are not into traditional furniture. They're more interested in contemporary-style furnishings. So this was a nice break in my woodworking. Normally the stuff I build is either out of pine or oak, and to use more traditional woods such as walnut and mahogany was a pleasure."
>
> ANDREW McPHERSON

Three Views

Another new direction for this craftsman began with finding a book on Colonial Williamsburg reproductions (The Colonial Williamsburg Foundation). It had been tossed into a dumpster—by some frustrated woodworker, perhaps?

The original design, so says the caption, was inspired by an English rococo tool chest of the late 1700s. Colonial mansions (and smaller abodes) used these fine furniture pieces to store tools for fixing up this old house before it became a "this old house." In today's homes (and in Andy's), it has returned as a silver/service chest.

Although he usually does not build reproductions, Andy refers to this catalog as a resource of past design. The Williamsburg Gentleman's Tool Chest, with some modification, was finally made for his home and this collection.

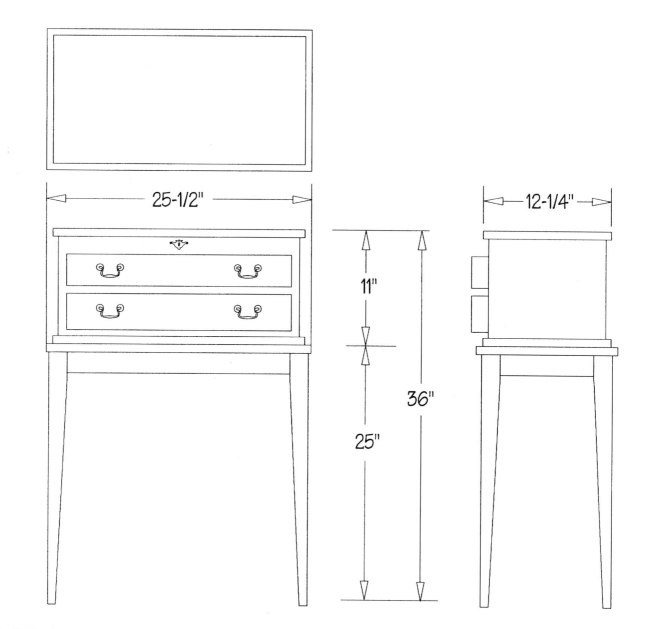

Design Details

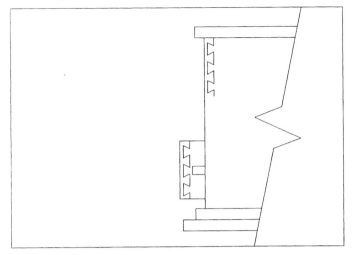

Machine-cut, half-blind dovetails join chest corners as a design. The walnut drawer faces provide high contrast definition to the oak drawer sides.

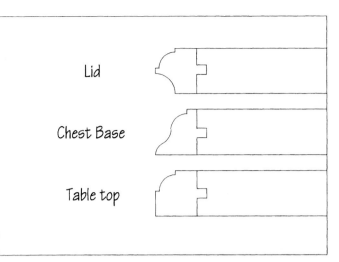

A couple of passes with the shaper nets molding profiles for the lid, with its slight lip for lifting and an ogee to create transition from the chest to tabletop. The tabletop edge has a lower relief, since it is most vulnerable to bumps and knocks.

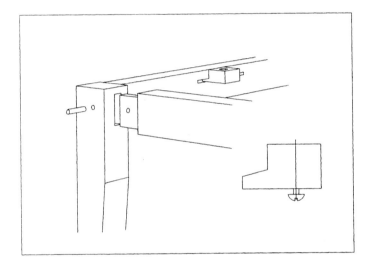

Inside tapered table legs attach to the apron in mortise and tenon joints. They are pinned with a walnut dowel to lock the joint and add a subtle design feature on the table. The top is fastened with L-clips fit into a dadoed slot along the inside edge of the apron. It is then screwed and glued to the underside of the tabletop. Even though it's MDF and won't expand and contract, Andy can't break old habits.

Williamsburg Gentleman's Tool Chest

Work in Progress

One wide board selected for the face nets the natural pattern, color and figuring overall, including drawer faces. He figures the reduction in height from the multiple kerfs and buys long to realign the natural pattern after losing the kerf widths.

A more substantial set-up than the one shown in the four-drawer project, mechanical dovetails are quicker and easier than hand-cut. They add their own distinctive look to the corners.

If you happen to have a hollow mortise/tenoner, plunge-cutting mortises for apron tenons makes quick work of an otherwise labor-intensive chiseling task.

Prepare veneer for covering the MDF top. Veneer on any surface can be adhered with contact cement. Whether this is superior to or equal to other veneering methods is still in deliberation.

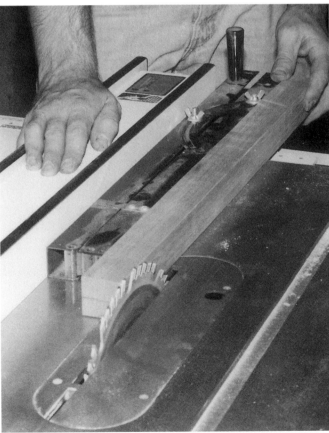

When discussing my clobbered-together taper jig, Andy asked, "Why build one, when the commercial versions are inexpensive?" Good point.

Note the continuous figuring of the walnut across rails, stiles and drawer faces in the finished chest with dovetail detail on case corner and drawers.

Variations

A tool chest that is more at home in the shop than the dining room can be designed to fit the tools of your trade or hobby, whether that be carver, shipwright, wheelwright, furniture maker or whatever. You can customize the drawers and trays for the contents.

As a variation to the finer side of furniture, you might consider a chest in oak or pine, with drawers, drop front above, lift-out tray covering a false bottom above the drawer casing. Bale handles could be added, or the sides could be built up with some relief. Perhaps they could follow the middle drawer line for not-too-serious moving about.

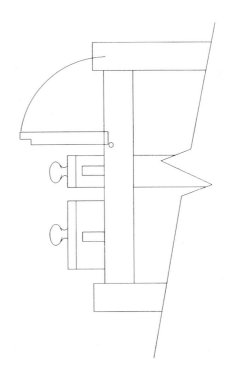

The Builder's Thoughts

Andy is immersed in woodworking, as shop owner crafting custom furniture, as a finish carpenter converting closets into entertainment centers, as a student still taking classes at Palomar College to expand his abilities, and as a sales rep for a local woodworker's supplier.

Hand-rubbing the finish on the inside tray enriches the applied finish.

Questions and Answers

Q What were your objectives for building this piece?
A I came across a book years ago, and in it was a certain chest that always inspired me—just the beauty and petiteness of it. It was a piece I wanted in my home, so when you were asking people to build chests, I thought I would take advantage of the opportunity.

Q What was your initial design concept, your initial thoughts?
A I pretty much followed the design to the letter. I did dovetail the corners where the original had been covered with a veneer. I find that dovetailing is a very attractive joint and gives the piece more interest. Other than that, it's pretty close to the original.

Q Was this design similar to your present style?
A It was quite a bit different. It seems that most people on the West Coast are not into traditional furniture. They're more interested in contemporary-style furnishings. So this was a nice break in my woodworking. Normally the stuff I build is either out of pine or oak, and to use more traditional woods such as walnut and mahogany was a pleasure.

Q Do you consider yourself a furniture maker, artisan, craftsman?
A I really don't like the word "artisan." I consider myself a craftsman. Some of the pieces can actually be a piece of art, such as the Maloof-style rocker I'm making now, but deep down inside, I'm still a craftsman.

Q Are your designs primarily functional or primarily an art form?
A They really are both. When I meet with a customer, I find his needs and that takes care of the functional part. But when constructing, I'll think something might look better another way, or add a detail—build it more as an art form. The client has a unique piece and can say it's an original.

Q Obviously you have a leaning toward period furniture with this piece. Was this your first introduction to the style?
A I did an eighteenth century bookcase. I have always liked eighteenth century furniture. The simpler stuff. Chippendale is too ornate for me. I like simple, straight lines. I'm not into carvings or ornate curves. There are certain pieces that are too simple, like the Arts and Crafts. I don't go that far. I like something a little more organic, something that flows, a little more interesting. I'm probably right in the middle, somewhere between traditional and contemporary.

Q Any new methods used in joinery, materials, finishes?
A This was my first use of veneers. I normally work with solid wood, but thought this would be a good opportunity to try veneers, with so many flat surfaces I wanted to keep flat.

Q Why did you choose MDF (Medium Density Fiberboard) for the top surfaces?
A Basically for stability. It's not going to expand or contract with weather conditions, it is always a flat surface, and it takes glue or contact cement nicely—excellent for gluing veneer.

Q What is your favorite, or most used, tool?
A The band saw is probably the most used, the most versatile. Actually one of my favorite tools in the shop is the simplest—the scraper. I use that more than anything. You can shape with it, you can sand with it. It is so easy to use. I wish more woodworkers would use it. Being at The Woodworkers' Store, I find people are clueless about what the scraper can do. You think back to the carpenters of the eighteenth century, they didn't have sandpaper, so they used the scraper, or maybe shark's skin for the final sanding.

Q What is your next tool buy?
A A horizontal boring machine for doweling. They cost about $1,000, so I invented my own and it works quite well. I attach a router at the back and use ⅜"- and ½"-up-cut bits to bore the holes.

Q Any woodworking tips or message for the reader?
A I guess I would say take on new challenges. Don't continue to use the same routines, the same joinery. Expand your imagination, reach out and grab something you wouldn't normally grab. If you find you can't do it the first time, keep trying, and before you know it, you become an expert at it. That is how I work, and it works.

Eighteenth Century Federal Sideboard

ROBERT STEVENSON • CHULA VISTA, CA

> *"It's a relatively easy piece to build—if you take the time. The joinery may look difficult, but it really isn't."*
>
> BOB STEVENSON

Three Views

The Eighteenth Century Federal Sideboard, built in the style of Hepplewhite, may be beyond the upper range of chests as defined in this book. However, the old-world craftsmanship may be applied to traditional furniture projects you undertake—chest or otherwise.

The veneering process of past craftsmen is reflected in this piece. Master furniture makers long ago realized that highly figured wood taken from a burl or crotch of a tree was a rarity and should be shared by applying thin sheets of veneer from the flitch. It was usually used either as surface decoration (onlay) or inset (inlay) in their fine furniture. They also knew that this wood, by its nature, is reactive—grown under tension and therefore not as suitable as straight grain-lumber for gluing up into panels.

But they had fun with the veneering. In addition to veneering entire surfaces or sections, onlay patterns included cross banding, straight and reticulated stringing and even marquetry and parquetry design, as both surface decoration and as inlay.

Another tradition of Federal period furniture was the use of a primary and secondary wood, using more common wood for the underpinnings and the more "select" wood for exposed surfaces as either full panels or edge-glued onto the secondary wood.

SPECIFICATIONS

Construction: ¾" dovetail casework

Materials: Solid cherry case, doors and drawer faces; secondary woods: pine (bottom, back, dividers), holly (drawer sides/back), bird's-eye maple and cherry veneers

Height: 32"

Width: 60"

Depth: 21"

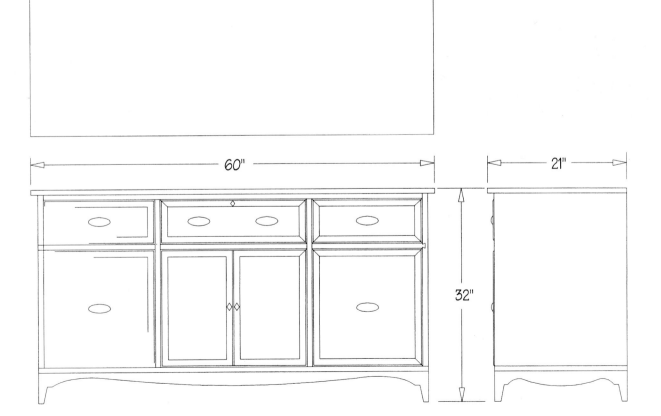

Design Details

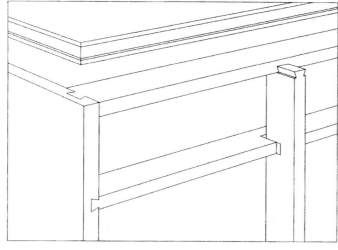

It's dovetail season. A 1″ × 4″ top brace receives vertical supports in sliding dovetails, which both supports the top and captures the sides with single dovetails let in at the ends. Drawer bearing rails and stiles are joined with sliding dovetails, and the cherry sides are joined to the pine bottom with half-blind dovetails.

The top is screwed on through slotted holes to allow seasonal expansion and contraction of the woods. Along the sides, L-clips are screwed into the top. They are captured in a dado slot along the sides, and slide with the lateral movement of the top and sides. With both top and sides oriented in the same cross-grain direction, everything should expand and contract the same distance.

The center drawer is ready for cock bead trim. Hand-cut dovetails joining drawer faces to sides are deep and nicely spaced, complete with the traditional scribed line marking dovetail length. Bead is cut narrow on the drawer sides to expose more dovetail.

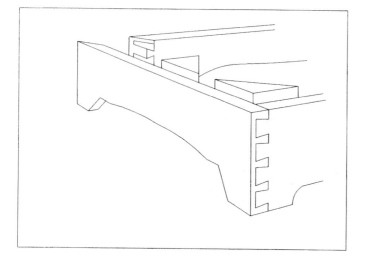

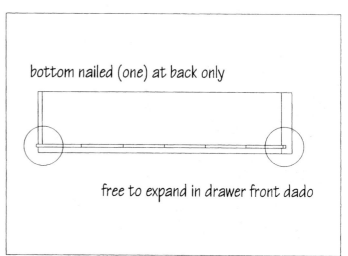

bottom nailed (one) at back only

free to expand in drawer front dado

The back apron is through-dovetailed (I told you it was in season) into the sides of the base. The bracket-foot corners in front are double-blind-mitered dovetails. Both are blocked from behind to bear the potential load.

The drawers are the English style. Bottoms are resawn, edge-glued pine with a rabbet planed around the edge to fit the capturing groove in the drawer sides and front. The ¼″ drawer bottom extends beyond and below the back, attached (with a single nail) at the back only to allow for seasonal cross-grain movement.

Work in Progress

A preparation reminder. A veneer saw will trim one side at 90°. The saw blade usually cuts a slight bevel on the trim side which needs planing back to a right-angle if this edge is to be butt joined.

A toothing plane flattens the gluing surfaces, the receiving piece (known as the ground) and the veneer flitch. In addition to flattening the glued surfaces, it cuts small grooves to increase the gluing area—a place for the hide glue to bond and hold.

Placing the veneer's good side into hide glue and spreading out over the receiving piece wets the face, while the glue is liberally applied to the gluing side. The veneer sheet is turned over and placed roughly in the center beyond all trim lines.

Applying hide glue to both sides of the veneer keeps both sides wet to prevent warpage and lubricates the veneer hammer while smoothing down bubbles and wrinkles.

The center panel is trimmed away around the drawer or door face using a cutting gauge set to the width of the crossbanding, with the flat side of the blade facing away from the fence for a 90° cut to butt against.

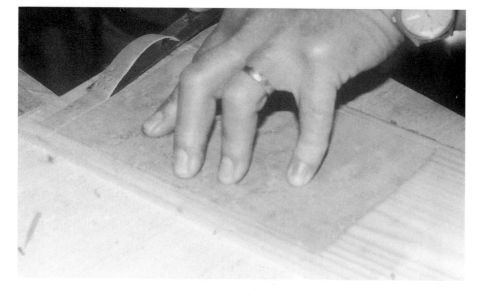

Remove trimmed excess. You need to work fairly fast before the hide glue sets, but you can, and will, re-wet the border for the next hide-glue application anyway. So, if the trim dries before removing, re-wet.

Hammer on the mitered, crossbanded border. This is where you would insert string banding if the design called for a framing band. For this design, the crossbanded cherry (grain runs across the narrow direction) butts against the center panel of bird's-eye maple. The mitered corners are cut before applying, but the width should overhang the edge.

The veneer is trimmed flush to the edges from the backside using a French veneer saw. The first pass lightly scores the cut line. Then tilting and pressing, but not creasing the veneer onto a cutting surface, make your cutting pass. The laminated edge will be rabbeted back and edged with cock bead trim.

Variations

A half-sideboard variation surfaced when Bob and his client first conferred on the design. Both appreciated a Hepplewhite half-sideboard pictured in *The Best the Country Affords, Vermont Furniture 1765–1850*, a catalog of an exhibition at the Bennington Museum, Bennington, Vermont, but agreed their project should be a full sideboard to nest inside a dining room niche.

For the variation, the half-design, or maybe a commode, are possible options, but whether you build a half-chest or full, consider following the construction used in this casework.

In whatever style you choose, the variation could include the primary and secondary wood approach, the top front brace to capture the sides, and sliding dovetails for the stiles.

In the two variations here, a small southwestern chest—a commode from a different time and culture—and a half-sideboard shown in a country style would be easier projects than a Federal (or any other) period reproduction.

This chest includes paneled doors (carved if you like), and geometric gussets set the southwestern style. For the country version, full-lapped drawers establish the front plane. Doors would lap the sides. Braces above and below the drawers could be mounted onto the sides to maintain that plane. The base could stand proud of the carcass to match the overhang of a tongue and groove or planked top. Panels inside door frames could pick up the tongue and groove pattern from the top.

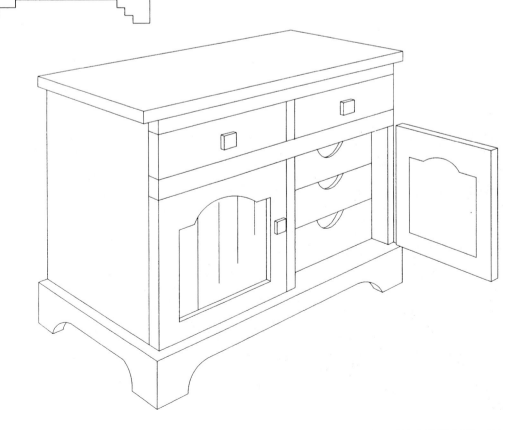

The Builder's Thoughts

Bob Stevenson has taken the chest to the extreme with his Hepplewhite sideboard. The intricate veneer work he used takes the sideboard from average casework furniture to work of art.

Bob Stevenson prepares a string band of ebony and maple for discussion and demonstration for an upcoming San Diego Fine Woodworkers Association meeting. Like the stringing, this demo was sandwiched between his deadline duties as Show and Exhibits Chairman for their next Design in Wood show.

Questions and Answers

Q Your willingness to be included in another book (Bob was profiled in *Earn a Second Income from Your Woodworking*) is appreciated. What were your thoughts on sharing your skills?

A That's what it's all about—teaching. I like to teach and I've done it for a long time, even when I was in medicine. It's just fun to share.

Q What was the initial design concept?

A The client needed a sideboard to go with her dining room table and chairs, but couldn't find anything of that period that would fit into a 6′ space. I first designed a more decorative piece that would have gone with her set quite well, and we went back and forth until we arrived at this style.

This one has a very simple string along the top edge and the bottom, which is the same string as is in her dining room table. We eliminated string around the door and drawer panels. I also proposed string on vertical legs—the legs were more prominent on the first design—and we just moved ahead making minor design adjustments.

The original layout of drawers and doors was her idea, and she wanted some sliding shelves and a couple other things. As we progressed the design kind of fell into place, removing some things she initially asked for and adding some things.

Q Was the design similar to your present style?

A Everything I do, and have done in the past, is done in traditional methods—hand-cut joinery. I don't use machines for joinery very often.

I have always liked Federal furniture. If I had the choice of making furniture, the Federal period would be the period I would choose to build it in—even the seating. Although I like making Windsor chairs, Federal chairs are kind of pretty. They are a little more delicate however, and they don't stand up as well as the Windsor.

Q How would you describe your design style?

A Most of my work is traditional. I have done some contemporary pieces associated with some classes in design. A desk I made out of claro walnut was a real departure for me, but I have restored a lot of Nakashima furniture, and that piece was made in his style.

Q Any major challenges in construction, materials, finish?

A Maybe the double-blind miter dovetails for the bracket-foot corners. I've done them before, but not a lot of them. It's always a challenge to get them nice and neat, but not that difficult.

Probably the hardest part was hammer veneering the door fronts. That's about the maximum that you can hammer veneer—about a 2′-square—because the glue sets so quickly. You need a press if you're going to do anything larger. In fact, the doors probably would have been better done in a press. Old-timers added urea (made from horse urine) to the glue, which extends open time. There's a fellow locally, Pat Edwards, making and bottling that glue, and it works quite well. You can actually use it in a vacuum press. The beauty of the hide glue is that it is totally reversible. You can repair it many, many times—even remove and re-glue the veneer.

Q Did you make your own edge band string?

A The only thing I didn't make was the string for this piece. The client was able to match it commercially. It's a very popular string of satinwood, ebony and holly. If it wasn't available commercially, I would have made it. In fact, I just got through making a sample for a demonstration I am doing. It's a rather interesting, but simple, way of making stringing.

In veneering, you have stringing and you have cross banding or edge banding, which in this case is cross banding. In cross banding, the flitch is cut across the grain to get either a straight or cathedral pattern by cross cutting plain-sawn (vertical grain) stock to expose the growth rings on edge.

One traditional veneering pattern is to put a string between veneers to make a border, a physical separation, around it. Stringing is a narrow band onlaid or inlaid to a piece. The term stringing refers to any single piece of decorative wood (holly or maple or ebony), or it could be multiple pieces put together in such a fashion to form a design repeated in a string.

Q And the edge banding around the top and base?

A This is inlay stringing, put into solid wood. Otherwise it would be just onlay stringing if it was put on the doors and drawers as surface decoration. Where it's actually in solid wood around the top and along the base of the cabinet, it is inlaid into a routed groove. In the eighteenth century method, they would have used a cutting gauge on both sides and used a mother's tooth plane to take out the inside recess.

Q What about drawer construction?

A I used basically an English-style drawer, and this is acceptable on this particular type of furniture because a lot of the cabinetmakers of that generation came over from England, or learned with English masters.

It's called an English drawer. The bottom slides in a groove dadoed in the drawer sides, or into mounts (cleats with dado groove pre-cut) attached to the drawer sides. The bottom has a tongue rabbeted along the sides and front. It is set into the front in a deeper groove, anywhere from ⅛″ to ¼″ deeper than the side grooves. This allows the drawer bottom to expand and contract. If you fix the bottom at the back end, the front can move in and out of the drawer front and never pull away.

Q Any problem milling the bead around the doors?

A I did that with an antique hand plane. It is a single-bead beading plane. I put a ³⁄₁₆″ bead on opposite edges of the wood, and then ripped the width on the table saw.

Q What is your favorite or most used tool?

A I have so many tools, I don't think there is any one tool that is my favorite. Mostly, I like and use the hand tools. The tools from the 1800s have generations of use already in them, and it's just a pleasure to use them.

Q What is your next tool buy?

A I'm a tool collector. I need two chisels to complete my set of Stanley Everlasts. (Any Everlasts out there?)

Q Any woodworking tips or message for a reader who might want to tackle a Federal sideboard?

A It's a relatively easy piece to build—if you take the time. The joinery may look difficult, but it really isn't.

One tip is to use a story stick. Putting your measurements on one piece of wood saves a lot of time. Once you have all of your measurements on a story stick, you don't need a measuring tape to actually build the piece.

Probably the best tip I could give in doing hand joinery would be to use marking tools that scribe a cut line, whether it be a cutting gauge, a marking gauge or knife. I never use a pencil. A pencil leaves too wide a line to follow. But a blade leaves a very accurate mark on the piece, and you can cut right up to either side of a really sharp mark.

INDEX

A

Alaskan Mill, 42
Armoire, as variation, 112
Art Deco, 22
Artistry. *See* Form vs. function
Arts and Crafts movement, 21-22
Ash, 60
Asian design
    influence of, 114
    joinery, 15
    tansu, 18, 59-64, 73-74

B

Band saw, 123
Bark, stripping, 41
Bauhaus, 22
Bearing frames, 85, 88
Bearing rail
    cutting relief in, 90
    and frame approach, 58
Biedermeier style, 21
Birch
    Finnish, 108
    veneer, 26
Biscuits, 39
Blanket chest, project, 35-40
    as variation, 49
Book-matching, 103
Boring machine, horizontal, 123
Bow-front design, 84, 89
    as variation, 104

C

Canopic chest, 13
Casework, 12, 17
    dovetail, 125
    veneered, 100, 108
Cedar, 38
    aromatic, 26, 36, 44
    chest, project, 43-49
    Spanish, 100
Chairside chest, project, 51-56
Cherry, 26, 52, 84, 125
    veneer, 84
Chest
    evolution of, 11-12
    history of, 13-23
    See also Projects, Semainier *and*
        individual names
Chests of drawers
    origin of, 12, 17
    project, 75-80
Chest-on-chest. *See* Highboy
Chisels, 106, 132
    Japanese, 114

Clamps, lightweight aluminum, 29
Cocobolo, 108-109
Coffer chests, 11, 17
Coin chest, project, 91-96
Collaboration, 98
Commode, 12, 17
    Dutch, 20
    elaborate, 19
Corner cleats, 77
Corners
    bracket "feet," 85
    dovetailed, 116
Coving bit, 87
Cowell, Ryan, 99, 105-107, 113-114
Craftsman style, 21, 52
    contemporary adaptations, 58
Cross banding, 128, 131

D

Dadoing, 55
De Stijl, 22
Deacon's bench, project, 25-31
Depth, as challenge, 74
Design concepts, original, 33, 41, 58,
    82, 105, 123, 131
Design details
    cigar humidor, 101
    coin collector's chest, 93
    Craftsman chairside chest, 53
    deacon's bench, 27
    drawer, 33
    eighteenth century Federal
        sideboard, 126
    Japanese tansu, 61
    lingerie chest, 85
    rustic blanket chest, 37
    Shaker chest of drawers, 77
    Williamsburg gentleman's tool
        chest, 117
Divider frames, 89
Dovetail(s), 33, 60-61
    with bow front, 84
    casework, 125
    corners, 116
    end-grain to end-grain, 74
    graduated sizes, 86
    half-blind, 117
    hand-cutting, 62
    Incra-Jig-cut, 77
    intermixing sizes, 82
    mechanical, 118
    sliding, 90, 109, 114, 126
    through, 126
Dowel holes, aligning, 55
Doweling, 53

Drawer(s), 17
    adding, 40
    curved, 85
    designing case to fit, 52, 58
    dry-fitting, 54
    English style, 126, 132
    height progression, 88, 90
    locking mechanism, 92-93
    origin, 12
    seals, 101-103
    vertical, 109
    See also Tray
Drawer bearer frames, 53
Drawer pulls, 87-88
Dresser, 17
    origin of, 12
Dry-fitting, 78
    dovetails, 62
    drawers, 54

E

Early America style, as variation, 31
Ebony, macassar, 100, 103
Edge, natural, rejoining, 37
Edge banding, 131

F

Face frame, assembling and gluing up
    flush with, 78
Federal style, 21, 124-132
    sideboard, 65
Fence, shop-made, 114
Filigreeing, 18
Finger joints, cutting, 48
Finish, 90
Flemish design, 16
Form vs. function, 34, 42, 50, 74, 82,
    90, 106, 123
Frame and panel design, 12
Functionalist Modern movement, 22
Furniture
    and architecture, marriage of, 22
    rustic, 36, 42

G

Gilding, 18
Gillis, E. John, 59, 73-74
Gothic style, 15
Grain direction, 27-28, 33
Graves, Garth, 43, 50, 51, 57-58
Greene and Greene, 58, 74, 114

H

Hambridge Progression, 88
Hammer veneering, 131

Hardware, 114
    Brusso, 108
    tansu, 61, 74, 96
    See also Drawer pulls, Hinges
Hepplewhite style, 20, 125
Hide glue, 127-128, 131
Highboy, 12, 17
Hinges, 93-94
    quadrant, 101
Holes, boring, for spindle pegs, 30
Holly, 125
Humidors, 76, 81
    project, 99-104

I
Incra System, 77

J
Japanese tansu, 73-74
    defined, 18
    project, 59-64
    as variation, 96
Jewelry chest, project, 107-112
Jig
    router, 85-86
    taper, 119
Joinery
    Asian, 15, 114
    beefing up, 74
    drawer, 63
    finger, 48
    gluing and bolting, 37
    half-lapped, 46
    mortise and tenon, 117-118
    See also Dovetail(s), Through-
        mortise tenons
Jointer, 38, 42

K
Knife, for marquetry, 98

L
Lag bolts, 37
Lid
    fixed, 12
    other uses of, 13
    planked, 11
Linenfolds, 16
Lingerie chest, project, 83-88
Lowlands design, 16-17

M
Mahogany, Honduras, 92
Maloof, Sam, 33-34, 74
Maple, 76

bird's-eye, 100, 108, 125
Marquetry, 92, 95, 98
McNeil, Gary, 91, 97-98
McPherson, Andrew, 115, 122-123
Medium Density Fiberboard (MDF),
    116, 119, 123
Middle Ages, 13
Milling, 42
    and keeping flat, 41
    for seal, 106
    special blade for, 42
Ming Dynasty, 15
Mission style, 21
    influence, 90
Molding
    to capture panels, 47
    roman ogee, 92
Molding rail, installing, 79
Morris, William, 21-22
Mortise and tenon joints, 117-118

N
Nail gun, tacking face frame with,
    78, 82
Newport School, 20

O
Oak, white, 44
Oriental design. *See* Asian design
Outgassing, 92, 100

P
Panel construction, 116
    See also Frame and panel design
Panels
    capturing, with molding, 47
    design of, 49
    dress-sanding, 58
    edge-glued, 60
    rabbeted, 48
Patterning bit, 87
Phyfe, Duncan, 21
Piechota, Stan, 58, 83, 89-90
Pine, 36, 125
    Jeffery, 38, 42
    logging, 36
    as variation, 56
Plywood, 108, 114
Pneumatic finish nailers, 82
Prevosto, Martin, 35, 41-42
Projects
    cigar humidor, 99-106
    coin collector's chest, 91-98
    Craftsman chairside chest, 51-58, 69
    deacon's bench, 25-34, 66

eighteenth century Federal
    sideboard, 124-132
Japanese tansu, 59-64, 70
jewelry chest, 72, 107-114
lingerie chest, 23, 68, 83-90
rustic blanket chest, 35-42, 65
Shaker chest of drawers, 68, 75-82
Spanish cedar chest, 43-50, 71
Williamsburg gentleman's tool
    chest, 69, 115-123
Pye, David, 74
Pyramid. *See* Roman ogee

Q
Queen Anne style, 19

R
Rabbeting, 61
    shaper, 102
Reed, Carol, 25, 32-34
Regency design, 19
Rhode Island School. *See* Newport
    School
Rococo design, 19
Roman ogee, 98
Router, 82
Router jig, 85-86
Router table, 90
Runners, gluing and screwing, 61

S
Sanding, with Shopsmith, 58
Sapling, cutting, 37
Saw. *See* Band saw, Table saw, Veneer
    saw
Scraper, 123
Seals, 101-103
    milled cedar, 106
Semainier, 88
Shaker style, 21
    adhering to, 82
    chest of drawers, 68
    as variation, 31, 40
Sideboard, project, 124-129
Six-plank design, 11, 16
Slabs, variations on, 40
Specialty chests, 91-132
Spindle peg
    boring holes for, 30
    cutting, 29
    hand cutting, 32
Splitting, avoiding, 12
Squaring-up, 28-29, 78
Stevenson, Robert, 124, 130-132
Storage chests, 25-50

Stump, hollow, as early chest, 11, 13

T

Tabbing fasteners, 114
Table saw, 90
Tallboy. *See* Highboy
Tansu. *See* Japanese tansu
Taper jig, 119
Templates, for hinges, 94
Thickness planer, 38, 42
Thickness sander, 106
Through-mortise tenons, 58
Tool chest, project, 115-121
Tools
    antique, 60
    marking, 132
    See also individual tools
Toothing plane, 127
Top. *See* Lid
Traupel, Mike, 75, 81-82
Tray
    compartmentalized, 94
    sliding, 109

V

Vacuum press, 106
V-block, chocking sapling in, 37
Veneer, types of, 92, 100, 108
    cherry, 84
    cherry and birch, 26
    walnut, 116
Veneering, 125
    book-matching, 103
    with contact cement, 119
    experience with, 105-106, 123
    and marquetry, 20
    See also Hammer veneering
Veneer saw, 127

W

Walnut, 116
William and Mary style, 19
Wood(s)
    air-drying, 38
    aromatic cedar, 26, 36, 44
    ash, 60
    bird's-eye maple, 100, 108, 125

cherry, 26, 52, 125
contrasting, 54
discoloration, 39
expansion and contraction, 53, 61,
    74, 85, 114
Finnish birch, 108
holly, 125
Honduras mahogany, 92
Jeffery pine, 36, 38, 42
macassar ebony, 100, 103
maple, 76
milling. *See* Milling
outgassing, 92, 100
pine, 125
Spanish cedar, 100
walnut, 116
white oak, 44
See also Medium Density
    Fiberboard; Veneer, types of
Wood-Mizer, 42
*The Woodworker's Guide to Furniture
    Design,* 57